FAMOUS FIREARMS
OF THE OLD WEST

PRAISE FOR *FAMOUS FIREARMS OF THE OLD WEST*

"Guns, like axes and hammers, can be useful. But only in certain hands do they grab our attention. Paul Bunyan's ax and John Henry's hammer have nothing on the guns wielded by fabled badmen and lawmen of the American West. From John Brown to Bonnie and Clyde, the frenetic decades between the Civil War and The Great Depression produced characters no master of fiction could imagine. They were also the most fruitful decades in firearms design. In *Famous Firearms of the Old West*, Hal Herring walks you through dusty corrals and into noisy saloons, waits with you on dark roads and leads you, horseback, reins in your teeth, through hailstorms of bullets. Telling of hard lives spent fast over fresh corpses, Herring hews meticulously to fact—the facts, at least, as they've been strained through legend. The photos are real, the references exhaustive. If you're a student of the gun and of a frontier defined by predators with steel in their hands, you'll find in these pages a whiff of nitrocellulose, and dying echoes of shots that shaped the American West."

—WAYNE VAN ZWOLL

"Most books on the old west only focus on the firearms of that period, the individual gunmen, or the cultural aspects of the western world. In *Famous Firearms of the Old West* Hal Herring has blended all three of these elements into one package, creating such a complete story of the weapons, the men wielding them, and the society they lived and killed in that you can almost smell the gunpowder in the air."

—TIGER McKEE,
DIRECTOR OF SHOOTRITE FIREARMS ACADEMY,
AUTHOR OF *THE BOOK OF TWO GUNS*

"Hal Herring has done an excellent job of combining the history of the firearms and the history of the people who used them in the Old West, so that the reader can learn about both in considerable detail. I'd recommend it as an addition to anyone's Old West library."

—MIKE VENTURINO,
STAFF WRITER FOR *GUNS, THE AMERICAN HANDGUNNER,
RIFLE,* AND *HANDLOADER* MAGAZINES

"Herring has written an amazing book! Gritty and compelling, *Famous Firearms of the Old West* tells the stories of real-life heroes, sinners, and cowards, and the guns that figured so prominently into their lives. A must-read for all lovers of guns and history. An amazing book!"

—BRIAN McCOMBIE,
SENIOR EDITOR, *GUNS & AMMO,*
AND COLUMNIST, *GUN DIGEST THE MAGAZINE*

FAMOUS FIREARMS OF THE OLD WEST

From Wild Bill Hickok's Colt Revolvers
to Geronimo's Winchester,
Twelve Guns That Shaped Our History

HAL HERRING

TWODOT®

GUILFORD, CONNECTICUT
HELENA, MONTANA
AN IMPRINT OF GLOBE PEQUOT PRESS

A · TWODOT® · BOOK

Copyright © 2008 Morris Book Publishing, LLC
First TwoDot paperback edition, 2011

The Library of Congress has previously catalogued an earlier (hardcover) edition as follows:

Herring, Hal.
Famous firearms of the Old West : from Wild Bill Hickok's Colt revolvers to Geronimo's Winchester : twelve guns that shaped our history / Hal Herring.
    p. cm.
Includes bibliographical references.
ISBN 978-0-7627-4508-1
1. Firearms—West (U.S.)—History. I. Title.

TS533.2.H47 2008
683.40978—dc22

2008010918

ISBN 978-0-7627-7349-7

Printed in the United States of America

10 9 8 7 6 5 4 3

This book is for my son Harold.

CONTENTS

ACKNOWLEDGMENTS

A book like this one is an attempt to boil down the knowledge, passions, and work of dozens of people, many of them no longer living. One of the real pleasures of writing a collection of true stories is to find the work of someone like Paul H. Wellman, historian and storyteller extraordinaire, whose books from *Death in the Desert* to *Dynasty of Western Outlaws* were standard references for me. I returned to them to read more slowly after my work was done, for the wonder of the stories he tells, and I suggest to any interested reader of this book that he or she do the same. Too many of the books that I consulted for this work fall into that category to be listed here; suffice it to say that Charles G. Worman (who is very much alive and writing, and graciously helped me) is the current dean of American firearms history, and his most recent book *Gunsmoke and Saddle Leather* is a treasure for anyone who loves guns, history, and photography. Bill O'Neill's *Encyclopedia of Western Outlaws* is another masterwork. Modernity calls for a new category of such works, and Frank R. Ballinger's Internet site Bonnie and Clyde's Hideout accomplishes that most difficult of tasks—allowing a visitor to inhabit and understand the lives and times of people long gone. Reading Bonnie Parker's poetry there, following links to newspaper stories written immediately after the robberies and gun battles, gazing at the huge archive of photos of men and women, their weapons, their families, gave me the chance to clear my head of the myths of the story, and ponder the more fantastic reality of it. Wyoming Tales and Trails, another brilliant Internet site, does the same thing for frontier Wyoming, and the story of Tom Horn.

My lifelong friend and shooting buddy Tiger McKee of Shootrite Firearms Academy gave me the run of the Shootrite library, and suggested that I include Texas Ranger Frank Hamer and his Remington Model 8 in my book.

Tiger's advice and help on this book, and in general, has been invaluable. Tiger introduced me to Mike Venturino, one of America's most prolific and learned gun writers, and Venturino was extremely generous with his time and knowledge. Almost every time I looked up a specific firearm on the Internet, Venturino would turn out to be the author of at least one of the articles. I spent hours poring over Winchester historian R. L. Wilson's comprehensive works, where seemingly no detail, of fact or photograph, has been left unexplored. His books are works of art.

I owe a debt of gratitude to all those curators and photo archivists that I tormented with telephone calls to obtain the photos used in this book. My sincere thanks to Ann Marie Donoghue, of the Buffalo Bill Historical Center, to Jason Schubert of the J. M. Davis Arms and Historical Museum, Chuck Rand of the National Cowboy Hall of Fame, Lou Stancari of the National Museum of the American Indian, Emily Lovick of the Fort Smith National Historic Site, Chris Gallo of Greg Martin Auctions, and Tracie Evans and Christina Stopka of The Texas Ranger Museum. No one was more helpful, and more patient with me than Bonnie Reynolds and the rest of the staff at The Museum of Church History and Art in Salt Lake City. Robert P. Palazzo, who knows more about gunfighters than I ever will, graciously sent photos from his collection, and gave me the benefit of his knowledge and storytelling for the price of a telephone call. James D. Julia Auctions in Fairfield, Maine, contributed the rare and beautiful photos of Tom Horn's revolver; the staff there is as excited by beautiful old weapons, and the wild histories behind them, as I am, and could not have been more gracious with their help. Robert McCubbin contributed the photos for the chapter on John Wesley Hardin, and his graciousness is much appreciated.

Finally, this book could not have been written without the office space provided by my friend Kurt Geise, who had to listen to most of these stories in monologue as he passed by my door trying to do his own work. His knowledge of guns old and new, and his willingness to offer his opinions, were a big part of this effort—not to mention the fact that he never pointed out the many times that the rent was long overdue.

PREFACE

The rifle sits in the glass case, and the museum is quiet, the fluorescent lights bright. It is merely an object of wood and steel; perhaps it is badly worn, or broken. The card below it describes why it is here, who owned it, what famous figure carried and used it. We linger over the exhibit mostly because the rifle belonged to someone famous, though some of us will make a careful study of almost any weapon—from war club to Hotchkiss gun to Apache helicopter or F-15—evaluating its efficiency, its weaknesses, imagining how it handles in battle, where it fits in the endless evolution of the mechanics of violence.

But, remember, there is a time and place, before the giant machines of war come to play, when the weapon and the warrior are inextricably linked. The term applied to these weapons is as old as conflict: *personal weapons.* Perhaps we take note of its wear patterns, a silvered place on the metal where a hand once gripped it, carrying it for months or years, or the reverse swayback on the fore stock, telling a story of a forward-heavy rifle resting, ready for hunt or fight, on the pommel of a saddle, polishing away the wood as the horse rocked across thousands of miles that are now covered by housing developments and the roar of cities. Here the bluing is gone to black from sweat, there the stock is stained with blood, here a man has etched the stock of his fighting rifle with a phrase or picture that meant something to him, or hammered brass tacks in the stock to make a cross or a sunburst. *Personal weapons.* Sitting hushed and immobile in museum cases, all lethal potential stilled, the blood dried, the cries silenced, the smoke blown away. They exist now as windows into the men and women who fought—righteously or not—and died, or were willing to die, with them. What they conjure up can be a powerful magic.

The rifle, or pistol, or whatever we are looking at, is also proof of something very elusive, something that often cannot be easily imagined.

This really happened.

Yes, there was a place where a Cherokee warrior and family man, hounded for a crime he did not commit, fought it out, over and over, driving off posses in furious firefights, moving through the woods near his home like a deadly wraith, never running, always ready. Or, there was a man who held to the old ways, and died, blasted by cannon fire, fighting to the end. And this is the rifle that put bullets into the bodies of his enemies. That front sight may have rested on a lawman's shirt pocket; those strange letters carved in the stock meant something to a decent man who could not be pushed and could not be taken alive. Look closely. Can you feel it? Do you know what it must have been like to be him?

And here is another weapon, a revolver, shiny and new-looking because John Wesley Hardin was shot down before he could wear it out with his endless practicing, the pearl handle always ready to protect a reputation for violence fading into years and cheap liquor. Can you smell the dust of El Paso, hear the clinking of shot glasses at the poker tables? There is a myth of Hardin, a dime novel Hardin, a movie Hardin. But there was a real John Wesley Hardin, too, and this pistol was his, carried in his hand, during long drinking nights, and days of trying to be a lawyer after a life of murder, combat, and prison. Still ridden hard by the demons of violence, but carrying a watch inscribed with words of love from his grown children, trying to write his autobiography, trying to be something else, something better, something he could not be. There's tragedy in that gun, if you look at it, and know the story.

It was the stories that brought me to this book. America was a nation born yelling, and in a cloud of black powder smoke. For most of its history, it has been the cradle of liberty and liberty means conflict. The American West holds the distinction of being one of those places where the definitions of America were forged. After the nation was founded, after independence and the Indian wars of the southeast, new generations of Americans poured from the relatively stable civilization of the East, to the anarchic new world created by the piecemeal destruction of the Native American hold on the plains and deserts. That new world, so dangerous, so pregnant with promise and heartbreak and brutal challenge, would change them—and our nation—forever, as surely as the crucible changes steel or glass. From then until now, our national identity has been closely tied to the experiences in that crucible. We are a free people, living by the fruits of our own labors in a land of both danger and abundance. The reality has changed. For better or worse, our definition of our country and ourselves has not.

The weapons in this book were primary tools of survival in that anarchic world that defined us, wielded in the service of evil, some of them, others in the service of righteousness; most were used in both. A few of these guns, like the rifle carried by Chief Joseph of the Nez Percé, were wielded with calculated ferocity, only after every other option had been crushed underfoot by an implacable and self-righteous conquering enemy. Great waves of history crashing over human beings make for great stories. I would never try to say that the story of guns is the story of America—it is far more complex than that. But the story of these guns sheds a very wide light on the history of our country, and the story of the men and women swept along by these historical tides, fighting with these weapons, now so quietly stored in museums. The men and women are us. These weapons are ours. The history cannot be changed. The more we know of it, the more stories we keep, the deeper and wilder our history becomes.

CHAPTER ONE

John Brown's Sharps Model 1850 Sporting Rifle

This rifle is unique in American history in that it is probably one of the first weapons to be chosen for deniability by its purchasers. It lacks many of the maker's marks usually found on Sharps and other brands of rifles. Its serial number of "60" means it was one of the first Model 1850s to be produced. Wealthy antislavery citizens, churches, and groups in the cities of the East Coast wanted to support and be a part of the bloody struggle in Kansas against proslavery forces who were trying to make the state a part of the Southern slaveholding empire. John Brown, austere, wind-burned and pious, pleading his case for money and arms in the salons and luxurious homes of eastern industrialists, personified the raw struggle for freedom on the prairies of Kansas. However, even his most fervent benefactors could see in his single-minded obsession and blazing eyes the potential for mayhem. Some of them believed Brown to be insane, even if his cause was just. The Sharps rifle made especially for Brown is one of the first examples of an untraceable firearm, offering his wealthy benefactors, insulated already by distance, another level of what is known today among politicians as deniability for whatever Brown might do. As it turned out, Brown's benefactors made a wise choice.

John Brown gave this Sharps to blacksmith and forge master Charles Blair of Collinsville, Connecticut, in 1859, as partial payment of a debt. Brown had contracted with Blair to produce the one thousand pikes he hoped to use to arm his slave rebellion at Harper's Ferry, Virginia. Always short of funds, Brown had trouble paying the $1,000 they had agreed on for the pikes, and it is believed that he gave this rifle to Blair as part of the payment before he undertook the disastrous Harper's Ferry Raid.

This Sharps Model 1850, .44 caliber, was specially made for abolitionist John Brown, and carried during the Kansas Campaign of 1856–1858; used in the Battle of Black Jack, the Battle of the Osawatomie, the Battle of the Spurs, and in many raids and skirmishes with proslavery militias in Kansas and Missouri, between 1855 and 1858; carried in the infamous Pottawatomie Massacre of 1856.

The rifle was obtained for the U.S. Cartridge Company's gun collection then passed into private hands. It was donated to the Smithsonian by Allen H. Johness Jr. of Metairie, Louisiana, in 1981.
Courtesy Smithsonian Institute

THE STORY OF THE SHARPS RIFLE

Since John Brown was captured and executed after his disastrous 1859 attempt to incite a slave uprising at Harper's Ferry, Virginia, it is perhaps ironic that the first breech-loading rifles, designed by Captain J. H. Hall in 1811, were produced at the same Harper's Ferry Armory. Gunsmiths and designers had been trying to find a way to evolve beyond the muzzleloader for obvious reasons: Muzzleloaders were almost impossible to load from horseback, and the fixed load of breech-loading rifles was more consistent, especially in times of battle stress, when soldiers handling muzzleloaders had been known to do everything from pouring half a flask of powder down their barrels, to ramming a ball in with no powder behind it at all, to any of a million terrified variations in between. Last but not least, a breechloader could be loaded while lying flat behind a small, life-saving roll of earth or other cover, while even the most professional operator of a muzzleloader had to expose himself to enemy fire to recharge his weapon. The Hall Breechloaders, models made in 1833 and 1843, saw much use in the Mexican War and on the frontier. They were still around and in use through the Kansas border wars of the 1850s, and into the earliest years of the Civil War, in the hands of Southern troops.

But the Halls were temperamental. The breech was crudely milled, and gas and fire often spurted from the gaps, close to the face of the shooter. Christian Sharps, born at the time of Hall's first patent in 1811, came to Harper's Ferry to work with Hall in 1830. Ten years later, working at his own Cincinnati, Ohio, gunworks, he took what he'd learned from the Hall and created the model for the first of the Sharps breech-loading rifles. It would be eight more years before he sought a patent for his new design.

The patent was for a breechloader that solved many of the weaknesses of the Hall rifles. Among the innovations: The trigger guard functioned as a lever that, pulled down and forward, moved a drop-block down, opening the breech for loading a sealed paper or linen cartridge. Bringing the trigger guard back brought the block up to seal the breech, and also cut the end off the cartridge, exposing the powder for ignition through a cap, or through the newer Maynard tape primers—basically a line of caps fitted onto a tape— or the R. S. Lawrence Disk Primer magazine—caps in a ring, like a modern child's cap gun. It is reported that although the seal of the breech on the Model 1850 Sharps were much better than anything produced by Hall, a small flash of fire still escaped when firing the weapon.

The first Sharps, like the one owned by John Brown, was made in .44 caliber. The model was produced, for only one year, for Christian Sharps by the factory of A. S. Nippes, in Philadelphia, Pennsylvania. The Model 1850 remains among the most rare of collectors' rifles—only about 150 of them were ever made.

The Model 1850 though, began the legend of the Sharps rifle that would continue through the Civil War and far beyond, to the end of the American frontier in 1881. The 1851s would see service against Apache raiders in Texas, and all along the Santa Fe Trail, as well as in thousands of other conflicts and in what may have been the era of the world's last, greatest hunting that accompanied the opening of the plains states. The "Beecher's Bibles" of the Bleeding Kansas era were mostly Model 1852s, or the Model 1853 Carbine in .52 caliber.

The Sharps greatest boom time, of course, would be the Civil War, when more than one hundred thousand of them were issued to Federal troops. Of these, most were carbines, forty-seven inches long, weighing eight pounds, and wonderful to handle on horseback. The most common Civil War cavalry rifle, the Sharps Models 1853 and 1855, became the sniper's favorite on both sides during the war. Those rifles and the models that followed them would play a major part in the Great Plains Indian Wars, and in the extermination of the buffalo. Sharps introduced a metallic cartridge rifle in the late 1860s (in caliber .50–70 Government), but many plainsmen and veteran warriors preferred the tried-and-true percussion guns, with their cheap linen patches and bullet molds, blocks of lead, and powder horns, the standard equipment of one of the world's wildest times and places.

POTTAWATOMIE CREEK, KANSAS TERRITORY, SUNDAY, MAY 25, 1856

It was as if, on this spring morning, the violent human ferment of the territory had been distilled down to its stinking, fly-blown essence, and displayed here beside a rutted wagon lane. Old Mr. William Doyle lay sprawled with his eyes open, a blue bullet hole in his forehead. His shirt was stiff with dried blood from the sword wounds in his chest. William Jr., twenty-two years old, was face down in the grass, his head split, jaw slashed open to the teeth, a wash of dark blood at one armpit.

When Mrs. Mahala Doyle found only the two bodies, she prayed that Drury, her twenty-year-old son, might have escaped the soft-spoken marauders who had come to their cabin in the dead of night. But while she and other settlers were getting ready to bury her husband and oldest son, the buzzards led them to Drury's body, hidden in the tall prairie grass. The sight of him, both arms chopped off, his fingers scattered around him where he must have been trying to protect himself from the awful blows of the sword, was almost too terrible to witness. He had been finished with a single sword-stroke to the heart. The Doyles had come to Kansas from Tennessee, where, they had told their new neighbors, there were no good jobs because slaves did all the work. William Sr. had been a proslavery man, even though he was far too poor to ever hope to own slaves himself.

When the men came at midnight to the Wilkinson homestead, Louisa Jane Wilkinson was so sick with measles that she begged them to return later to speak with her husband. She was afraid that if she were left alone, she might die of her illness. The night riders claimed to represent something called the northern army. The ramrod straight old man who led them was like a figure from a dream of the Old Testament, with the brush-torn clothes and dramatic white beard of a wilderness penitent. He seemed to be without, or beyond, anger; when he spoke to Mrs. Wilkinson, he was polite.

Jules Abels in his biography of Brown, *Man on Fire,* describes those dread moments, "You have neighbors that will help you," he said. The Wilkinson children, awakened and afraid, gathered around. Mrs. Wilkinson said that the neighbors lived far away. "It matters not," the old man said. When the armed men refused to let Allen Wilkinson put on his boots before leaving, she realized suddenly that they had come to kill him. She never understood why. He was a member of the proslavery Kansas legislature, but he had not been outspoken about his views. They were hardscrabble settlers, trying to make their way in the new territory, just like everybody else.

A neighbor, coming to check on her in her illness, found Allen Wilkinson's body, tangled in a brush pile near the cabin, stabbed, his throat slashed, his skull split above the ear.

William Sherman was taken from the cabin of his brother "Dutch Henry" Sherman, who was a ruffian, and sometime ferryman. Dutch Henry embodied many of the hatreds that infected the territory. He despised anyone who questioned the righteousness of slavery, or suggested that the Kansas Territory should be free of the practice. But Dutch Henry was safely away from home. The body of his brother William would be found at ten o'clock in the morning in the creek, his brains washed out of his cleaved skull.

John Brown and his sons, and a select group of militia, had changed the dynamic of the struggle in Kansas. The massacre of relative innocents in any struggle introduces flesh-and-blood terror in place of fiery rhetoric, bluster, or hollow armchair exhortations to fight. Terror abolishes the theoretical and replaces it with either silence or battle. Brown preferred the latter, and he got it.

THE STORY OF JOHN BROWN

When John Brown first entered the American consciousness, the year was 1855, and he was fifty-six years old. He had fathered his last child, Ellen, in 1854, with his second wife, Mary Anne (his first wife died in 1832, along with their three-day-old son), whom he had married when she was sixteen and he almost thirty-three. Brown had led his family on an odyssey from small New York State farms, to a failed but ambitious tannery in Pennsylvania, to more farms in backcountry Ohio. A wool-selling venture that ended badly once took him to Europe. He was a gifted livestock handler and breeder, but an indifferent businessman. His family was never hungry, but real financial success eluded him, which was confusing to a man who, it was agreed upon by all who knew him, held himself and his own intelligence in highest esteem. He was a biblical scholar and a great reader, spending what little time he had between work with biographies of Cromwell and Napoleon, or the classic Plutarch's *Lives*. Wherever he settled, he was known as much for his honesty and work ethic as he was for his piety and for his skill as a debater. The most famous ex-slave and abolitionist leader of the day, Frederick Douglass, described Brown, whom he met in 1847, as one of the few Americans he had ever known who lacked any semblance of racial prejudice, or even racial feeling. The idea that slavery existed in America had tormented Brown always; he considered slavery a vast sin that encouraged and contained a myriad of other sins, all growing like monstrous weeds, watered by the blood of innocents, cultivated with the kind of base cruelty that destroyed both men and nations.

The 1840s were particularly cruel to John Brown. He suffered bankruptcy and was jailed in Akron, Ohio, when he and two of his sons took up arms to try and prevent a foreclosure on their farm. He and Mary Anne lost four of their children to illness, and a toddler to a terrible home accident in which she was scalded to death. He and his family fought to survive on a pioneer farm in North Elba, New York, where the growing season was barely three months long, but the population of freed slaves living in the area provided Brown with near endless opportunities to teach, and mingle with, a people for

John Brown—farmer, wool merchant, Biblical scholar, philosopher, murderer, and warrior—in his extravagant championing of abolitionism, helped push America toward Civil War.

Library of Congress, LC-USZ62-106337

*Frederick Douglass was born a slave in Maryland, escaping north to freedom
in 1838 at the age of twenty, eventually becoming one of abolitionism's most
effective and articulate voices. His bestselling autobiography,* Narrative of the
Life of Frederick Douglass, An American Slave, *remains one of literature's
most powerful arguments for human rights. Douglass met John Brown in 1847,
and later described him as one of the few Americans he had ever met who
lacked any semblance of racism.*
Library of Congress LC-DIG-cwpbh-05089

whom he felt great respect and responsibility. At North Elba, he spent most of his money buying winter clothes for the ex-slaves, who were not well prepared to survive the howling blizzards of the Adirondack Mountains.

By 1855 he abandoned his efforts at business and farming, and took up a new calling as a self-described instrument of God, destined to strike a blow against the institution of slavery. Five of his sons were already in Kansas, on homesteads in the southeast corner of the state near the community of Osawatomie. In 1855 John Brown Jr., following the latest invasion by Missouri border ruffians into Kansas, wrote to his father that "the interest of despotism has secured to its cause hundreds and thousands of the meanest and most desperate men, armed to the teeth with Revolvers, Bowie Knives, Rifles & Cannon . . . the friends of freedom are not one fourth of them half armed . . . the result of this is that the people here exhibit the most abject and cowardly spirit. Now we want you to get for us these arms. We need them more than we do bread." John Brown Sr. wasted no time. He gathered a small amount of money from local abolitionists, a case of rifles, ten old broadswords, and a supply of warm clothes. He left his wife and children on the farm at North Elba, in the warmth of the brief summer, and headed west for Kansas, picking up his sixteen-year-old-son Oliver in Detroit on his way.

The Kansas Territory, opened for settlement in 1854, was called Bleeding Kansas by 1855. It was a name that would stay with it until the outbreak of the Civil War, when the nation as a whole would claim the adjective. In the middle 1850s, Kansas was the scene of dozens of killings wrought by proslavery and antislavery, or abolitionist, elements alike. Until John Brown's massacre of innocents on Pottawatomie Creek, the fighting had been sporadic, a warming war of attrition, testing the limits of lawlessness. In the year that followed Pottawatomie, more than two hundred people would die in the conflict.

Most Southerners supported the adoption of slavery into the new state. Their support was strengthened in Kansas by the legions of border ruffians, lawless men who claimed allegiance to the South, or at least to Missouri. (Senator Charles Sumner of Massachusetts called the border ruffians "hirelings, picked from the drunken spew and vomit of an uneasy civilization.") Abolitionists, called "Free-Staters" in Kansas, argued that none of the newly opened Great Plains states should embrace what they considered to be the most destructive and repulsive institution in the United States, contrary to every notion of Christianity, human decency, and the ideals of America. Caught in between was a third group that opposed the adoption of slavery to the new state (after all the homesteader's ethic was of liberty through radical self-sufficiency) but did not argue for abolition elsewhere. This group learned to keep their mouths shut, or be attacked by both sides.

> ## "I did not come to Kansas to settle. I came to fight."
> —ABOLITIONIST JOHN BROWN

The conflict allowed for a general lawlessness to prevail, and antislavery settlers as well as border ruffians often used the ferment as an excuse to raid homesteads for livestock and other spoils. (A raider's cry: "There is a proslavery cow! Take it!") Typical of these times, perhaps, was twenty-four-year-old William Clarke Quantrill, the former schoolteacher, and future Southern guerilla leader. Quantrill robbed and murdered abolitionists and proslavery settlers with equal aplomb. Raised in an abolitionist family, he occasionally rode with the fanatical abolitionist Kansas Jayhawkers and Redlegs, stealing and killing deep into Missouri. Weeks later, he would be seen with proslavery militias like the Kickapoo Rangers, doing the same in Kansas. He lived in Lawrence, and in the saloons, camps, and flophouses along the rivers, where he sometimes made money catching and reselling runaway slaves. When he needed a place to rest, he holed up in the camps of the Delaware Indians, under an alias, and claimed to be a detective.

The slavery issue was boiling hot, across the entire United States, with the Underground Railroad well established and Northern newspapers and churches calling daily for slavery to be abolished once and for all. It was one of the strange tricks of history that the prairies of Kansas would become the first battleground of the Civil War. Neighboring Missouri held fifty thousand slaves. With an avowed abolitionist government in Kansas, and a population of settlers committed to Underground Railroad activities, Missouri slaveholders could foresee the end of the institution in their state. Senator Atchison of Missouri said, "If Abolitionism is established in Kansas, there will be constant strife and bloodshed between Kansas and Missouri . . . Negro stealing will be a principle and a vocation. It will be the principle of philanthropic knaves until they force the slaveholder to abandon Missouri." (Atchison would soon cross to Kansas and found the town of Atchison, headquarters of the militant proslavery newspaper the *Squatter Sovereign.*)

As slavery in Missouri fell, so Southerners said, the expansion of Southern influence over the West would halt, and the last of the slave states would become even more besieged by the great weight of abolitionist pressure in the North. The fate of the South, it was believed, rested on a proslavery Kansas.

The abolitionists believed that, too, and hoped to use the state to drive a knife into the South. Inspired by the fiery speeches of East Coast religious leaders like the Reverend Henry Ward Beecher (the brother of Harriet Beecher Stowe, author of *Uncle Tom's Cabin*), abolitionists set up the New England Emigrant Aid Society, sponsoring settlers who went to Kansas strictly to join the beleaguered antislavery cause. These settlers held no illusions about what they were coming to Kansas to accomplish. They brought with them the newest breech-loading Sharps rifles (most of them Model 1852s), made in Hartford, Connecticut, bought for them by the congregations of churches in Connecticut, or by the parishioners of Reverend Beecher's Plymouth Congregation Church of Brooklyn, New York. The Sharps rifles were packed in cases marked BIBLES and were known, especially to the border ruffians and proslavery men, as "Beecher's Bibles." At one point Missourians blockaded the main travel artery of the Missouri River, boarding all boats and searching the belongings of all would-be Kansas settlers. Many Sharps rifles were confiscated in these raids, but many others, concealed under loads of grain, in pianos, disguised as crates of farm implements, made it through.

The question asked of any new settler, and indeed, any man met on the roads of Kansas was the code, "How do you stand on the goose?" The proslavery answer was, "I am sound on the goose." Any answer could get you killed.

Politically, the proslavery elements of Kansas had held the power since November of 1854, when hundreds of armed Missourians had flooded across the border to cast their votes for proslavery candidates in the Kansas Territory. In March of 1855, the process was repeated, this time with even greater numbers of Missourians, as many as five thousand men, controlling the roads and trails of the region, terrorizing Free-Staters at the polls, and casting 6,307 votes to elect an entire legislature of proslavery candidates. Since the Kansas Territory held only 2,905 eligible voters at the time, it was obvious that something was amiss. The new legislature wrote a complex Black Code, legalizing slavery, denying rights to blacks, and making it a crime for any citizen to speak against slavery, or even to discuss the issue in any but a positive light. Free-Staters, of whom many, but not all, were abolitionists, held elections and established a government of their own, centered in the town of Lawrence. Intertwined business and political interests in the territory used the border ruffians as their strong-arm men to try and hold the Free-Staters in check. U.S. President Franklin Pierce was ultimately responsible for ensuring that free and honest elections, as guaranteed by the Constitution, were held in every territory and state, but when Kansas's territorial governor Andrew Reeder asked for help from the president, citing the massive voter fraud and impending violence, Pierce simply replaced him with Wilson Shannon, a proslavery loyalist.

Border ruffians held the abolitionists and Free-Staters in contempt, as did their puppets and paymasters, the Southern businessmen who had taken over the government. It was believed that these "bleeding-heart nigger-worshippers"—even those well armed with "Beecher's Bibles"—lacked the backbone for a real fight.

John Brown joined his four sons in Kansas in October of 1855 to prove that belief wrong. Across the pommel of his saddle, when he had a horse to ride, or in his right hand, when he was destitute and afoot, he carried his own .44 Model 1850 "Beecher's Bible," specially ordered for him by his wealthy abolitionist benefactors in Connecticut.

Brown rode into Kansas, in a wagon full of armaments, carrying his Sharps rifle at the ready, a .31 caliber revolver (made by the Massachusetts

Arms Company) in his belt, a broadsword near at hand. The wagon had six upright posts, and on each was fixed a bayonet, pointing skyward, that could be removed with a flick of the wrist. His sons rode either with him or on horses at his side. They had met with James H. Lane, an antislavery militia leader, known as The Grim Chieftain of Kansas (who included among his fighters a young William Hickok, not yet known as Wild Bill), and they had ridden south, forsaking the safety of the abolitionist stronghold of Lawrence, for the anarchy of the rolling grasslands and forests of the border near the settlement of Osawatomie. Jules Abels recounts what John Brown would tell almost anyone who asked, "I did not come to Kansas to settle. I came to fight."

At first he and his sons and their small band of armed abolitionists found few opponents. When they heard rumors that a band of two thousand Missourians, armed with cannon, were poised on the Wakarusa River to attack the Free State capital of Lawrence, they rushed there, bringing in the wagonload of arms. John Brown was made a captain of a twenty-man company in defense of the town. James H. Lane and others entered into a peace treaty with some representatives of the Missouri invaders, infuriating Brown, who screamed that he "spit on it" (the treaty) and that given a minimum of support, he and his men would immediately attack the invaders on the Wakarusa and send them packing. Brown had to be forcibly subdued. Lane and many Lawrence citizens believed that his plan was suicidal, both for him and for the town and its people. But Brown had made a name for himself.

The Browns endured one of the worst winters they had ever witnessed, the prairie wind and cold beyond anything that the Adirondacks had ever shown them. The weather brought hostilities to a halt until January 15, when a band of cabin-fevered Kickapoo Rangers, a proslavery militia, captured a Free State settler and hacked him to pieces, carrying the mangled corpse through the countryside in a wagon to show anyone who would look at it, before returning it to his wife by throwing it through the door of her cabin. A series of murders followed, including that of the proslavery sheriff Samuel L. Jones near Lawrence. The proslavery legislature, which was the recognized body of law in the territory, convened a grand jury that declared that the

Free-Staters were guilty of treason and subject to arrest. Among those indicted were James H. Lane and former governor Andrew Reeder. The Free State Hotel of Lawrence was declared a public threat, as were two Lawrence newspapers that were written by Free-Staters. It was time, wrote the *Squatter Sovereign,* to clean out the "seditious fanatics of the crack-brained town of Lawrence." It was May 20, 1856.

The Kickapoo Rangers showed up first, soon joined by several hundred armed men, three hundred of them settlers brought to Kansas from Alabama. They marched on Lawrence to carry out the commands of the law. Lane and Reeder escaped. The citizens of Lawrence sent appeals to Governor Shannon, but the governor replied that he would not "interpose to save them from the consequences of their illegal acts." The militias met no resistance, and helped themselves to the spoils of the town, including plenty of liquor. The Free State Hotel was burned to the ground; homes were pillaged and burned. When the militia left the wrecked town, its members were in a high state of joyous abandon.

It is widely believed that the sacking of Lawrence, and the passivity of the citizens there, drove John Brown to lead his sons and other militia members to commit what would be called the Pottawatomie Massacre on May 24. It is possible that Brown also had learned of the incident that took place on May 22, in the halls of Congress where South Carolina Senator Preston Brooks had beaten antislavery Senator Charles Sumner of Massachusetts, with a gutta-percha cane, causing Sumner injuries that would require almost three years to heal.

Whatever the impetus, Brown and his men committed one of the more terrible crimes of the conflict. In a revealing quirk of history, Northern abolitionists would use Brown's later heroism and his stern and unyielding courage as object lessons for their cause, ignoring the Pottawatomie Massacre entirely. It was not until 1879 that Northerners acknowledged that their hero had led and participated in the killings.

After the Pottawatomie murders, Brown, four of his sons and a dozen of his men, including militia leader Samuel Shore, went into hiding out in the thickets of a creek bottom. They would wait but two days for the powder keg that they had lit to explode. On May 27, a militia composed of Alabama and Georgia fighters rode to seek out the Pottawatomie killers. They struck Brown's settlement at Osawatomie and burned all the buildings to the ground, taking the cattle and other stock. John Brown Jr., caught by surprise, was captured hiding in the woods some twenty miles from his lost homestead. Jason Brown, who abhorred violence, and had taken no part in the massacre—in fact he would call it a vicious and inexcusable crime for the rest of his life—was captured by the Reverend Martin White, the leader of a band of border ruffians from Missouri. Jason's life was spared. John Jr. suffered, but was not killed. Instead, his hands were tied, and he was lassoed tightly with a long rope, and driven on foot by a mounted rider, at a fast trot, for almost twenty miles, a march that almost killed him. Once the militiamen arrived at their camp, John Jr. was beaten unconscious. The countryside was rife with reprisal killings. (John Jr. would later be freed on bail; Jason was released.)

Capt. Henry Clay Pate, graduate of the University of Virginia, newspaper correspondent and author, captain of the Missouri militia, and a deputy U.S. marshal led a band of eighty men from Missouri to arrest Brown and his abolitionist murderers. For all of Pate's seeming accomplishments, he was actually a twenty-four-year-old novice in the art and craft of war. He led his men to a pleasant camp in a shady grove of Blackjack oaks, and settled back. On the morning of June 2, as the men were cooking breakfast, Pate was astonished to see a band of about twenty ragamuffins, their clothes in rags, beards and hair wild, appear on foot across a small ravine from his camp. The leading ragamuffin, an old man, hatless, with a huge white beard, aiming a Sharps rifle, suddenly gave the command to fire.

The fusillade was terrible. Pate's men returned it as best they could, but managed only to wound Brown's son-in-law, Henry Thompson, with a bullet through the lungs. Thompson never stopped shooting. Brown's fellow militia leader Samuel Shore abandoned the fight after the first volley, and disappeared with his followers. Pate and his men took shelter behind their wagonloads of provisions, and heard Brown command his men to direct their fire at the Missourian's horses, which began to scream and fall. Then the Brown men returned their withering fire on the Missourians themselves. Pate would not know until after he and twenty-nine of his men surrendered (the rest fled), that Brown had only nine men with him at the finish of the fight. He had been confused by a galloping figure in the woods behind him, a wild man with matted yellow hair, who rode back and forth screaming, "Father! Father! We have them surrounded!" Later Pate and his men would learn that this strange horseman was Frederick Brown, John Brown's sixth child, a sturdy young man who suffered from insanity, and who could not be trusted with a gun. Frederick had broken away from his brothers during the heat of the fight, and made his own crazed version of an assault from the rear. It had worked, even if it had been accidental.

According to Abels, Pate would say much later, "I went to take Brown, and he took me."

The news of Pate's defeat traveled fast. Newspaper correspondents from as far away as New York City sought Brown out in his thicketed lairs. They called the Pate fight the "Battle of Black Jack" and wrote the story of the Puritan warrior, the furious saint with the Sharps rifle and the prophet's beard, the Leonidas of the prairies.

Free-Staters came in from all directions to join him in the thickets. Provisions, guns, powder, and lead were plentiful, and augmented by raids on proslavery homesteads. One Kansas legislator said, of both the Pottawatomie Massacre and the subsequent Battle of Black Jack, "It vertebrated the free-state party."

And the tide began to turn against the proslavery elements and the Missouri border ruffians. Brown rode north to join forces with James Lane, and to let some of his sons, exhausted by fever, wounds, or the hard living, escape Kansas. By August 20, he led a militia of thirty hand-chosen and well-armed men. There was a tremendous amount of raiding undertaken by Free-Staters at this time, and no one seems to know how much of it was done at Brown's command. But the proslavery forces seemed to feel his awful presence everywhere. The *New York Times* called John Brown "the terror of all Missouri," even though his raids were mostly confined to Kansas.

The Reverend Martin White, who seemed to have an uncanny ability to find the Browns, shot and killed the deranged Frederick Brown as he rode alone to join his father. Reverend White was in the advance guard of several hundred Missourians who were invading Kansas to wipe out the Free State militias. The force intended to start with another, and this time final, assault on the settlement of Osawatomie. Brown and his men were camped on the Marais des Cygnes River, across from the settlement, and they prepared for the defense. Brown told one of his men, who had not yet seen combat, "Take more pains to end life well than to live long." It would be at least 250 seasoned Missouri fighters, mounted and equipped with artillery, against Brown's thirty men. Again, Brown and his son Jason, who had so far avoided killing anyone, led the fight. Spread out forty yards apart and well hidden, the Free-Staters poured fire onto the mounted Missourians. The pro-slavers' cannon fire exploded in the trees around them, too high to be effective, although Brown was knocked down by a piece of grapeshot that ricocheted from a shattered tree. But the Missourians were sent into disorder by the accurate fire from the Sharps, coming from seemingly nowhere, and from an unknown number of adversaries who seemed, perhaps, with all the religiosity common to the Southerners, to be aided by a higher power. The commander of the troops ordered them to attack on foot, and they rushed forward into the thickets. Brown and his men made an orderly retreat, stopping to wound the Missourians who tried to follow them across the Marais des Cygnes. The Missourians proceeded with their plans to destroy the thirty or so homes of Osawatomie, and take all the provisions that Brown and his men had raided from proslavery settlers. The commander of the Missourians reported that he had killed "Old Brown," his son, and thirty of his men. In truth Brown lost six men, with four wounded, and inflicted more casualties than that on the vastly larger force that had opposed him. When proslavery newspapers were forced to admit that Brown and Jason were not, in fact, killed, and that the tiny force had once again proved itself against fantastic odds, the Missourians and their allies in Kansas lost any credit for their victory. Old Brown was the hero, referred to more and more as "Osawatomie Brown."

The fighting and raiding slowed. Federal troops moved in to try and restore order. A new assault on Lawrence by proslavery forces and border ruffians dissolved into nothing. Though he would return to Kansas several times until early in 1859, John Brown moved on to new battles, not least a triumphant series of fund-raising lectures in the abolitionist hotbed of Boston, where he would secure the funds for his long-dreamed of slave rebellion. The scions of church and industry who sponsored Brown had always been wary of him, afraid of his fervor, afraid that, rather than the fierce light of righteousness burning in his eyes, there might be something else, a fire of madness or mania. Perhaps they were correct.

Brown was captured at Harper's Ferry, on October 16, 1859, after his bloody attempt to start a general slave rebellion disintegrated. His sons Oliver and Watson, among many other people, would die in the fight there. Brown was hanged at 11:15 on the morning of December 2, 1859. The entire nation, North and South, had been transfixed by John Brown's trial, following his every eloquent and fiery utterance in the newspapers of the day. At the time of his death, at 11:50, church bells began ringing in Northern cities from Boston and New York and out to the Kansas plains. It is often said that however he is judged by history, Brown accomplished his one stated goal: to precipitate a war against the institution of slavery.

CHAPTER TWO

James Butler "Wild Bill" Hickok's
Colt Model 1851 Revolvers

The two ivory-handled Colt Model 1851s on display at the Buffalo Bill Historical Center in Cody, Wyoming, were almost certainly the property of James Butler "Wild Bill" Hickok, when he was murdered in Deadwood, Dakota Territory (now South Dakota), on August 2, 1876. Both were believed to have been purchased by private individuals—for twenty-five cents each—in an auction of Hickok's possessions that was held to pay his burial expenses. Of the two, the pistol showing more wear was kept as a general purpose farm gun in South Dakota for many years. It was used primarily to deliver the coup de grâce to hogs on their way to market and table.

These Colt Model 1851 Revolvers, .36 caliber, Percussion (Cap and Ball), ivory handled, were engraved at the Colt factory by master engraver Gustave Young. They carry serial numbers: 204672 and 204685.

The revolvers are on loan to, and on display at, the Buffalo Bill Historical Center, Cody, Wyoming.

Courtesy H. Sterling Fenn
LII.85.1 Courtesy Private Lender

According to Buffalo Bill Historical Center curator and historian Dr. Judy Winchester, the revolvers came to be identified, and loaned to the collection, in an odd and roundabout way. "We['ve] had the first pistol on display since 1969," Dr. Winchester said, "and the history on it was that it was bought at the auction, for twenty-five cents, to help pay Wild Bill's burial expenses." Winchester continued: "Sometime in the early eighties, a visitor came by to ask our curator where it came from. He thought that because we are the Buffalo Bill Center, that it must have belonged to Bill Cody." When the curator told him that the Colt was believed to be from Wild Bill Hickok in Deadwood, the visitor said that he suspected as much because he had the match to it, bought in Deadwood, for twenty-five cents, at an auction to pay Wild Bill's burial expenses! The serial numbers of the two identical Colts were only thirteen numbers apart, beyond coincidence for a revolver whose last production serial numbers ranged to 215,000. Both pistols have an engraved "E" following the numbers, indicating that they were engraved at the Colt factory, rather than after purchase. Although Dr. Winchester remains cautious—she is a veteran of disputed weapons and museum controversies—the Colts on display are also identical to those shown in one of the most famous photos of Wild Bill Hickok ever taken.

It is remarkable that, of all the histories written about Hickok, the origins of these highly distinctive Colt Model 1851s has never been established. Although he carried and fought with the Model 1851s almost exclusively, such beautiful weapons were unlikely to have come out of the tumult of the Civil War, or the hardscrabble guerilla battles of the Missouri Border Wars where Hickok honed his lethal craft. The brace of pistols may have been given to him by the antislavery senator Henry Wilson of Massachusetts, who hired Hickok as guide for him and his friends in a trip through the wild Arkansas River country in 1869, as a bonus for a trip that was considered, by all, a wonderful success. Others believe that the Union Pacific Railroad presented the ivory-handled revolvers to him as a lawman's reward for bringing order to the intolerable melee of Hays, Kansas. Whatever their origins, if they came into his possession as early as 1869, they were the primary tools of many a violent conflict, in the hands of one of the West's most skilled gunfighters.

The Story of the Colt Model 1851

There had been handguns around for centuries, from the smooth bore flint locks jammed in the belts of the early pirates to the horse pistols—giant (four and a half pounds loaded) Walker Colts and Model 1848 Colt Dragoons—so-called because they were best carried in a scabbard on a saddle. There were the tiny, 1848 "Baby Dragoons," too, true pocket pistols, concealable and great for surprise attacks or as a last resort at close range, even if, at .31 caliber, they were woefully underpowered for actual fighting. But it was the Colt Model 1851 Navy in .36 caliber that truly brought the handgun into the age of the gunfighter. It was the world's first real holster pistol, perfectly suited for carry, rugged, reliable, and extremely accurate in the right hands.

It was called the "Navy" across the West, probably due to the naval warfare scene—a fight between Texas ships and the Mexican Navy—inscribed on the cylinders on the first run of 1851s produced, a kind of thank you to the U.S. Navy for purchasing a large shipment of Colt Paterson Revolvers for their sailors, a purchase that had rescued the often cash-strapped Colt company. The navy, too, held the .36 as their standard caliber, while the army of the time still required pistols of .44 caliber. The ubiquitous Navy became a standard tool of the western frontier, just as it became the standard tool of close range warfare in the Civil War. Southern general Robert E. Lee carried a Model 1851. So did Richard Francis Burton, the English explorer, warrior, and spy (he spoke twenty-nine languages) who fought his way through bandits to reach Mecca (disguised as an Afghan tribesman) in 1853. So also did a wide host of less scholarly characters, from the James Gang to Plains Indians and everybody in between. By the time the model was discontinued in 1873 to make way for cartridge guns, a quarter million of the pistols were in use across the United States. The Civil War—and especially the Border

Wars—had taught a vital lesson to every combatant: A six-shooter in each hand, operated with skill and ruthlessness, represented overwhelming firepower for the time. The Colt Navy, the 1851 in .36, was not the most powerful handgun around. Loaded with a conservative twenty-five grains of black powder, it would push an eighty-six-grain ball to almost one thousand feet per second, hitting with the force of a modern standard .38 special, around 120 foot-pounds of force. Looking at old photos of the Missouri Border War fighters, and reading the accounts of the men who rode with William Quantrill, where a single fighter, well mounted on a strong horse, carrying a rifle and as many as half a dozen Colt Navies in holsters strapped to his body, could break cavalry charges and wreak havoc on large bands of regular soldiers not as well prepared, is to understand how the cult of the gunfighter as an artist of violence evolved and flourished. The Navies were an integral part of that flowering, so loved, and so tough, that many of them were actually converted to cartridge guns in the 1870s, to see service on into the twentieth century. The most famous artist of the Colt Model 1851 Navy would not live to see that, however.

THE STORY OF WILD BILL HICKOK

Some people called him a "frontier dandy," even a "fop" (a truly dreaded appellation in a time when "fancy" was among the worst insults available), for his habit of taking frequent baths and wearing a soft, finely made, fringed pale buckskin shirt. His pants were well tailored, his boots of the finest leather. He kept his long hair combed out, and he was clean-shaven as often as possible. Around his waist he wore a brilliant red sash, tied tight, perhaps to accentuate his narrow waist and add drama to his swagger through the mud and dust of the cow towns. But the red sash always held two Colt Model 1851s, carried grip-down, for the cross-draw that he favored, and that lightning motion was the last drama that many would-be killers and violent hell-raisers ever saw. Before he was thirty years old, James Butler "Wild Bill" Hickok had become the so-called Prince of Pistoleers, a legend in the dime

James Butler Hickok was born in Illinois on May 27 of 1837 and died in Deadwood, South Dakota, on August 2, 1876. The years between were filled with experiences almost equal to the myth. He worked as an abolitionist, a Union scout and spy, U.S. Army scout, lawman, gambler, and gunfighter, living through some of the wildest days of the Wild West.

Printroom.com

novels and the magazines of his time, his exploits blown outward into the realms of the surreal. But no one who ever knew him doubted that, under the hype, beyond the finery, Hickok owned the ferocity and ruthless calm of a born gunfighter, a man tested in every kind of combat, and found more than equal to the task.

Hickok was born to an antislavery family in Troy Grove, Illinois, on May 27, 1837. His father was a deacon of the Presbyterian Church, and the Hickok family farm served as a stop on the Underground Railway, ferrying fugitive slaves to freedom. As a youth James was a part of these smuggling efforts—certainly, the times were dangerous for his family, and he was encouraged in developing his skill with rifle and pistol, fists, and knives.

Although courtly and polite to a fault, he displayed early a stolid unwillingness to back down from any kind of fight. During one of his first paid jobs digging canals, he got into a fistfight with a youth named Charles Hudson and beat him almost to death, prompting Hickok to flee Illinois and begin the peregrinations that did not end until the drunken coward Jack McCall shot him in the back of the head, for reasons unknown, in Deadwood, South Dakota, in August of 1876.

It was as a Union scout and spy in the Civil War that Hickok would truly come of age as a gunfighter, in the fieriest and most brutal crucible of that conflict: the black-flag combat of the Missouri and Kansas Border Wars. At the outbreak of hostilities in 1861, the twenty-four-year-old Hickok had already lived a legendary existence in the West, fighting Indians and driving freight wagons for the Pony Express with Buffalo Bill Cody, who became a lifelong friend. After being mauled by a grizzly bear on Raton Pass in southern Colorado (he was found pinned beneath the bear, having killed it with pistol and knife), Hickok was sent to Rock Creek, a stage station in Kansas, to recover from his wounds. There he ran afoul of David C. McCanles, a quick-tempered young businessman who ran a competing freight line. McCanles hated Hickok (there are rumors that Hickok courted McCanles's mistress, a woman named Sarah Shull) and called him "Duck Bill;" to make fun of his profile, and "hermaphrodite." The isolated station was full of discord. Ready to fight one afternoon, McCanles called for Hickok (who was still limping and weak from the bear attack) to come out of the house of station manager (and Hickok's boss), Horace Wellman. Hickok waited for McCanles to try and enter the house and shot him dead. Two of McCanles's employees rushed the house, and Hickok shot them both. The wounded men were followed and finished off, one of them by Mrs. Wellman, the stationmaster's wife, who chopped the man to death with a hoe.

After the war began, Hickok rode for the Union both in the regular army and with the forces of "The Grim Chieftain of Kansas," James Lane. In both capacities he rode as a civilian scout and spy, fighting against Rebel regulars and the Southern guerilla bands run by men like Bloody Bill

Anderson and William Quantrill. He disguised himself as a Rebel and rode with Rebel bands, luring them into traps, reporting on their movements, equipment, and plans. The fighting was classic guerilla warfare: fast-riding clashes in the shadows of the forests, horse-born duels in hayfields, blistering attacks and counters on isolated farmsteads. When fighting slowed along the border, he fought as a regular in some of the most decisive battles of the war, most notably at Pea Ridge, where he earned distinction as a sniper. He would say, years later, that in his first major engagement, the disastrous (for the Union) Battle of Wilson's Creek, he had been terrified to the point of paralysis. It was probably during these war years that he first began carrying the Colt model 1851s—the weapon of choice for the border fighters, on both sides. It was during these violent and anarchic years, too, that Hickok developed the personal style—the double draw, double fire—that has been so commonly seen in Western movies, but was actually rare, requiring unique skills, among them the ability to aim either pistol with both eyes open, and both eyes equally dominant. It was reported by his traveling companions, among them famed names like Gen. George A. Custer (for whom he rode as a scout and Indian fighter after the Civil War), Colorado Charlie Utter, and Bill Cody, that Hickok maintained a rigid daily practice with his 1851s, shooting every morning before breaking camp. He was a completely ambidextrous shooter, as deadly with left as with his right, a true rarity.

The origin of the name "Wild Bill" has as many explanations as there were fables about the man during his life. One of the most credible is that the name was called out in thanks by a woman in a crowd in Independence, Missouri, after Hickok had faced down a lynch mob using his double 1851s, during the Border Wars. Others say that it was given him for his daring deeds as scout and spy. However it came to him, it was the legendary Wild Bill Hickok who would kill seven men in personal combat with pistols, not James Butler, and it was Wild Bill that stood as a two-gun lawman and quelled the two most dangerous towns in the Wild West of the late 1860s and early 1870s: Abilene and Hays, Kansas. Often, it was said, Hickok could still the rowdiest crowd, or halt a furious fight, simply by declaring loudly, "Alright, this has gone far enough!" He was on duty when eighteen-year-old John Wesley Hardin rode into Abilene at the end of a long cattle drive from Texas, at the height of Hardin's hell-raising and man-killing years. Instead of confronting Hardin, Hickok befriended the youth, helped him get his partner out of jail for a murder charge, and spent hours drinking wine and gambling with him.

Among the gunfights that involved Hickok's Colt Model 1851s was the August 1865, "high noon" style duel with former soldier (some say Union, most say Rebel) and battle-hardened Arkansas gunman Dave Tutt, in Springfield, Missouri. Tutt and Hickok had both been courting a woman named Susanna Moore. Debts from a card game at the local Lyon House tavern created further tension between the two men, with Tutt claiming Hickok's prized pocket watch as part of a disputed gambling debt. After threats back and forth, they met in Springfield's town square at about six o'clock in the evening. Tutt drew his pistol and fired from almost seventy-five yards away, an epic distance with a handgun. Hickok fired almost simultaneously, steadying his right-hand-gripped Colt 1851 with his left hand, and taking a steady aim. Tutt's bullet missed. Hickok's bullet went straight through Tutt's heart and killed him. Hickok then faced Tutt's gathering friends, now holding both his Colts at the ready. There were no takers for that fight. A jury acquitted Hickok of murder.

His last years were troubled, his wanderings almost ceaseless. Old wounds, including an Indian lance wound through his thigh, troubled him. He drank heavily and disliked working, and despite his outlandish fame, fueled by a stream of articles in popular magazines, he was often penniless when his gambling luck went bad. A sojourn in the East with Buffalo Bill Cody's Wild West Show was derailed by Hickok's drinking, and his view of the show—and his part in it—as ridiculous. Glaucoma—or perhaps a condition called ophthalmia related to gonorrhea—dimmed his eyesight. In an 1871 gunfight in Abilene, Kansas, he killed badman Phil Coe, but in the riotous aftermath, he shot and killed his own deputy, a man named Mike

A memorial at Hickok's birthplace, Troy Grove, Illinois
Library of Congress, LC-DIG-ppmsc-02687

Williams, who was rushing through the crowd, pistol in hand, to help him. Hickok apparently never quite reconciled himself to that accident. As far as anyone knows, he never killed another man. Also, his killing of Phil Coe, a well-known Texas cowboy and hell-raiser, while entirely justified, would haunt Hickok in another way: More than a few Texas gunmen swore to avenge Coe, and a heavy purse was apparently waiting as a reward for the first man to do so.

Hickok married Agnes Lake on March 5, 1876, when he was thirty-nine years old. Lake was a widow (her husband was shot to death), eleven years older than Hickok. She was possessed of no particular physical beauty, but was a former lion tamer and acrobat, and the owner of the Hippo-Olympiad and Mammoth Circus. The marriage mystified many, but the affection between the two seemed genuine. Hickok left his new bride after two weeks to try and build a stake for their lives together by gambling in Deadwood, Dakota Territory, at the height of the Black Hills Gold Rush. According to his friends at the time, White Eye Jack Anderson, Colorado Charlie Utter, and Calamity Jane, Hickok was despondent and paranoid, with constant presentiments of his own doom. A losing streak at the card tables of a dozen different bars—he moved constantly through the town, either out of restlessness or to avoid enemies—left him in debt.

The dread and feeling of doom turned out to be well warranted. His killer, Jack McCall, was a man of no distinction, who may have been hired by local enemies of Hickok, or may have owed Hickok money from a card game. No one ever knew. McCall would later say that Hickok killed his brother in a scrap in Abilene, which was yet another of his lies, since he had no brothers. McCall, seeing that Hickok was seated in a chair with his back to the exit of the barroom, crept up behind him, drew a battered .45 Colt revolver, and shot him. The bullet passed through Hickok's brain, exited his right cheek, and lodged in the wrist of fellow card player and riverboat pilot Frank Massie, who would carry it the rest of his long life. According to most accounts of the killing, McCall yelled, "Take that!" after Hickok hit the floor. He then tried to shoot the bartender, but the old .45 misfired. McCall was initially found not guilty of murder in a sham trial in Deadwood and fled the town, but his bragging and drunken claims of killing Hickok in a fair fight eventually led angry lawmen in Wyoming to arrest him. He was hanged for the murder at Yankton, South Dakota, in 1877, claiming the unenviable honor of being the first man hanged in the brand new state.

CHAPTER THREE
William "Buffalo Bill" Cody's
Springfield Model 1863 Rifle

The Springfield Model 1863 was used by Buffalo Bill Cody in many engagements with Plains Indians during his years (1868–1872) as a scout for the U.S. Army, and as a commercial hunting rifle, to take over 4,280 buffalo in an eight-month period ending in May of 1868, while Cody was employed as a contractor supplying meat to the twelve hundred workers of the Kansas Pacific Railroad, then under construction across Kansas. The rifle was also used in the famous buffalo-shooting contest between Cody and William Comstock, also sometimes called "Buffalo Bill," near Oakley, Kansas, during which Cody won the right to use the name for himself. Cody may have taken this rifle from the U.S. Army when he left its service after the Civil War ended in 1865. He named it Lucrezia Borgia after the murderous and beautiful

This .50–70 Springfield "Trapdoor" Model 1863, Second Allin Conversion, missing its shoulder stock, engraved on the lock plate with the date "1865," and the name "Lucrezia Borgia," was donated or sold to the Buffalo Bill Historical Center sometime around 1951, and remains on display there. This is what's left of her.

A .50–70 Springfield exactly like Lucrezia Borgia but intact
Photos Courtesy Buffalo Bill Historical Society, Cody, Wyoming

Italian noblewoman in the Victor Hugo play *Lucrezia Borgia* that had played in theaters as far west as Leavenworth, Kansas, during the Civil War.

SOMEWHERE ALONG THE SALINE RIVER, KANSAS, OCTOBER 1868

On such level plains, a man on horseback could see for a long way. Unfortunately, he could be seen for just as far. It had been a successful morning's buffalo hunt, with fifteen killed, and the wagon creaked and groaned under the weight of huge buffalo hams, humps, piles of purple-rich backstraps, and pale tongues. The roll of hides in the back of the wagon was drying and stiffening in the wind as the afternoon light shifted. Scotty, the butcher, drove the wagon, his rifle propped against the seat, two revolvers at his waist, two more in holsters beside him. Buffalo Bill Cody rode ahead on a borrowed horse, the forearm of his long .50–70 Springfield resting on the pommel of his saddle, its wrist held in his right hand. The rifle was a part of him, like an extension of his arm. He had won his name of Buffalo Bill with it, had made his wages killing meat for the army and the railroad, had fought off and killed Indians with it. He called it Lucrezia Borgia, after a murderous and beautiful woman character in a Victor Hugo play, *Lucrezia Borgia,* that he'd seen in St. Louis, on a night that seemed a world away from these windy flat grasslands, crisscrossed with raiding parties of Cheyenne and Comanche and ruthless white plunderers who followed no law of man or nature.

A brace of Remington .44 pistols hung over Cody's saddle horn; two more were jammed into his belt. Only a few weeks before, caught out alone, he had barely managed to outrun a dozen Cheyenne warriors, surviving only by the deceptive stamina and speed of his own horse, Brigham, and a few well-placed shots from Lucrezia Borgia, taken at full and desperate gallop. One of the shots had killed the lead pursuing horse, striking the beautiful animal dead center in the forehead and sending its Indian rider in a wild rag doll tumble across the grass.

For the past few days the prairies had been still but for the movements of the ancient herds: pronghorn, mule deer, elk, buffalo. Sandhill cranes poured over in wide arcs high above, going south. But Cody knew the silence around him was an illusion. And he knew that when it broke this time, with a wagon and only one fast horse for two men, running would not be an option.

The Cheyenne came riding out of the head of a ravine that led down to the Saline River, a war party thirty strong, armed to the teeth and well mounted. Cody saw the lead riders suddenly turn their heads to look at this strange apparition of a loaded wagon, with no escort of soldiers, lurching along through their territory. There was no hesitation. The column of raiders turned like a snake and attacked in mass, whooping and yipping and snapping their quirts against the flanks of their horses.

It was a sight and sound that was the last for many a plainsman, many a wagon master or family dreaming of the rainy farmlands of Oregon. But Scotty and Buffalo Bill Cody were a different breed of plainsmen. The plan had been made weeks before. Scotty leapt from the wagon, tied the mules, and began throwing out the buffalo hams—any one of which weighed over a hundred pounds. He was a small man, wiry and strong, and he heaved and dragged the hams into place as breastworks around the wheels of the wagon. Cody tied his horse and leapt down to help, bringing with him the weapons, the revolvers, rifles, and boxes of cartridges. The first bullets began to *thunk* into the meat, to clang against the metal fixtures of the wagon, and splinter the wooden sides. The mules screamed in pain as bullets and arrows found them. The two besieged men opened fire with their rifles first, saving the revolvers for the inevitable close-quarter fight ahead. At one hundred yards a raider flew backward off his horse, center-shot in the sternum with the 550-grain lead bullet from Cody's rifle. Working the trapdoor on the Springfield, Cody loaded another round while Scotty opened up with his revolvers. In his autobiography, Cody would later call their efforts, "a sudden and galling fire."

The raiders slowed and circled, firing, but wary of the cool marksmen beneath the wagon. It had all looked so very easy only moments ago. They charged again, this time braving the fire to fifty yards, where suddenly two of them fell dead. Cody knew that if the raiders wounded either him or Scotty, the hole left in the defense would spell death for them both. He fired his rifle, rolled to the back of the wagon, and testing to make sure the wind was carrying away from them, struck a match and set fire to the autumn-dry grass. The fire, driven by the wind, poured across the prairie, throwing a whirl of heavy smoke skyward. It was another facet of the survival plan—Cody had an agreement with the soldiers at the railroad camp to come looking for him if they saw smoke. The Cheyenne retreated to a small elevation some distance away, dismounted, and lay down on the grass, peppering the wagon from afar. Cody and Scotty managed to kill two more of them, shooting at the raiders' heads as they lifted them above the grass to take aim. When the soldiers appeared on the horizon, the raiders mounted their horses and galloped away. The soldiers helped Cody and Scotty reload the wagon and hitch a replacement team to it. The two plainsmen were uninjured. They reported that the meat was fine, too, except for the bullets and arrows embedded in it.

THE STORY OF THE "TRAPDOOR SPRINGFIELD"

The rifle that William Buffalo Bill Cody called Lucrezia Borgia was what he called a "needlegun," a common appellation in the 1860s West for any gun that used a firing pin rather than a percussion cap. (The real needleguns, of course, were the German Dreyse Model 1848s that used a needlelike firing pin and a paper cartridge, an early breechloader that was used in the 1866 Austro-Prussian War and other conflicts of the time.) Technically, Lucrezia Borgia was a .50–70–425, meaning it had a fifty-caliber bore, and fired a 425-grain bullet (often uploaded to a 550 grains for heavy game) propelled by 70 grains of black powder.

The 1866 Model Springfield was the result of a hyperspeed evolution occurring in firearms, drawing on the American experience of four years of the most intense use of weapons, in every conceivable kind of engagement, that the world had ever seen up to that point, the American Civil War. As early as 1865, thousands of the muzzle-loading .58 caliber Springfield 1861

The only known photo of Buffalo Bill with his famous rifle, Lucrezia Borgia, which he named after a beautiful and murderous woman in a Victor Hugo play.

Courtesy Buffalo Bill Historical Society, Cody, Wyoming

and 1863 muskets, fresh from the battlefields, went to the factories of the North for a radical conversion. The rifles were milled out to convert them into breechloaders that would fire a new, odd, rimfire cartridge of .58 caliber (.58–60–500). The Federal armorers, weighted with the experience of the war, knew that the future lay with the breechloader and a loaded metallic cartridge. The question remained as to what that cartridge would be, and what breech-loading system would best utilize it when it was developed. For this exploration a call went out from armorers and the U.S. government to gun designers all over the world to submit their plans and ideas. The 1865 conversion—spearheaded by inventor and master armorer at the U.S. Springfield Armory, Erskine S. Allin—was called the "First Allin Conversion," and resulted in the Model 1865 Springfield, with the breech that opened from the top for loading, known forever more in history as the first "Trapdoor Springfield."

The first "trapdoor" had a few weaknesses—chief among them were too many small moving parts—but Allin simplified and strengthened the design over the course of the next year. The .50–70 cartridge was also developed during this time, the first centerfire cartridge adopted by the U.S. military (it would remain the standard military cartridge until 1873, when the venerable .45–70 would replace it). The new "Second Allin" conversions were produced as the Springfield Model 1866, also called the "trapdoor" and soon to make history as they were deployed against the Plains Indians. On August 2, 1867, a force of thirty-one U.S. Army soldiers led by Capt. James Powell were protecting a large crew of civilian employees who were cutting timbers to build and reinforce Fort Phil Kearny, along the Bozeman Trail (north of present-day Buffalo, Wyoming). The soldiers were equipped with the new Model 1866 Springfields, Second Allin Conversion, in .50–70 caliber, which had been recently supplied after studies of the Fetterman Massacre of December 1866, where eighty-one troops equipped with muzzleloaders, a few Spencer carbines, and .44 Henrys (with their underpowered cartridges) had been wiped out by Oglala Sioux warriors under Crazy Horse and other chiefs. The Fetterman Massacre involved the unsuccessful protection of woodcutters, a fact that the Fort Phil Kearny soldiers would all have known. Before noon on that hot August day, in the shadow of the Bighorn Mountains, as many as two thousand Sioux warriors under Red Cloud attacked the woodcutters and Captain Powell's guard. While the soldiers responded to the initial rush, the civilians raced to pull the fourteen wood wagons into an oval around them all. What followed would go down in history as The Wagon Box Fight—five hours of relentless combat and siege, the Springfields firing continuously in what must have been a rain of arrows and bullets. The battle cost the lives of only five soldiers before reinforcements arrived and Red Cloud quit the field. What had seemed like a certain victory for the Sioux had become a bloodbath. Scattered in the grass were the bodies of 60 warriors, with at least 120 more badly wounded. There is no record of how many Sioux horses were lost in the fight. The new breechloaders (in the hands of courageous and disciplined soldiers) were widely credited with the success of the defense, as were the heavy .50–70 loads that could reach far and strike with a devastating effect that made the .44s fired by lever-action repeaters like the Henry or the Winchester Model 1866, look like a handgun.

Such ballistics, efficient loading capability, and reliability changed the dynamics of warfare and hunting on the Great Plains. One of the most extreme shots in Western lore was made with the .50–70 (fired from a Sharps rifle, some accounts make the cartridge a .50–90) by Billy Dixon, following the four-day Second Battle of Adobe Walls near Amarillo, Texas, in 1874, when Indians from several plains tribes, enraged at the slaughter of the buffalo, unsuccessfully attempted to wipe out a team of hide hunters at a fortified trading post. A group of the hunters were gathered together at a break in the battle, celebrating their survival, when Indian horsemen appeared on a far bluff. Dixon, a noted marksman, was encouraged to try to kill one of them with his "Big Fifty" as he called it. Dixon fired at the riders, and an Indian tumbled from his horse. The distance was later estimated to be fifteen hundred yards. Such a shot is improbable—"harassing fire"—at best, but it is possible. Loaded with the standard seventy grains of black powder, the 425-grain bullet of the .50–70 travels at 1,448 feet per second, and retains enough energy, even at fifteen hundred yards, to kill if it hits the right place. The epic shot made by Dixon is believed to have demoralized the attacking Indians and caused them to abandon the fight.

THE STORY OF BUFFALO BILL

Buffalo Bill Cody never said exactly where he obtained Lucrezia Borgia, though it is possible that he took the rifle with him when he mustered out of the U.S. Army at the close of the Civil War. At that time he was still simply Billy Cody, twenty years old, who came very late to the Civil War because he had made a promise to his mother that he would not enlist as long as he was needed to work and support her and his family. When the widow Cody died in 1863, Billy went to war. In all his life of outlandish fame, he almost always downplayed or made a joke of his real adventures. Explaining his enlistment, he would write that after a bout of very bad whiskey, he awoke to find himself a soldier in the Seventh Kansas, bound for battle. By all accounts he served admirably in combat and as a scout, spying and carrying messages far behind enemy lines, where he also ran into his old mentor and fellow veteran of the Bleeding Kansas days, Wild Bill Hickok, who was engaged in the same work for the Union Army. The two men would be lifelong friends, and cross paths from the darkest days of the Indian Wars to the bright lights of Cody's Wild West Show to the mud and blood and gambling halls of Deadwood, where Hickok met his end.

Billy Cody was born near Leclair, Iowa, on February 26, 1846, to a reasonably prosperous farming family. His father, Isaac, was a man drawn to the frontier; as soon as Iowa was thoroughly tamed, he began dreaming of Kansas. When Billy's brother Samuel was killed while galloping his horse home from school, grief set the family on the wagon road west, and they were among the earliest arrivals in the Kansas Territory. Leaving his wife and daughters with his brother Elijah, a storekeeper (and slave owner) on the border at Weston, Missouri, Isaac and eight-year-old Billy, who was already an accomplished horseman, rode deep into Kansas, stopping at Fort Leavenworth. In his memoirs Buffalo Bill would describe that day as one of the greatest of his life. The

COLONEL W. F. CODY

Pony Express rider at fourteen, Union soldier at seventeen, professional hunter and U.S. Army Scout at twenty-two, Medal of Honor winner at twenty-six, showman extraordinaire, William Frederick "Buffalo Bill" Cody came from a hardscrabble abolitionist homestead on the Kansas plains to be the most famous showman of his time, touring the world and amassing a fortune that he mostly gave away.

Library of Congress, LC-USZ62-118316

fort was packed with soldiers waiting for orders to ride west and try to subjugate Brigham Young and his Mormons, who seemed to have taken over Utah for their kingdom. Indians of every tribe, from Choctaws to Kickapoos, were trading and drifting through, or pausing to cook fresh venison over smoky fires. Fur trappers and traders rode among and with them, men as wild and free as any who have ever lived.

The family settled in the Salt Creek Valley, building a makeshift cabin, close to the freight lines, wagons, and oxen, all going west. They prospered. Like the family of Wild Bill Hickok, the Codys were Free-Staters, meaning that, while they may or may not have supported the abolition of slavery in the South, they wanted Kansas to remain free of the practice. Proslavery Uncle Elijah had set up a new store in the Salt Creek Valley, and it became a gathering place for men of like mind. One June morning in 1856, Billy and his father rode to Elijah's store to pick up their pay for a load of wood and hay that Elijah had sold for them. A small mob of proslavery men was there, drinking and working themselves into a frenzy over the politics of the new territory. They accosted Isaac Cody, accusing him of being an abolitionist, and pushing and shoving him. Isaac would not back down, and one of the men, an employee at the store, leapt forward with a long knife and stabbed him in the back. Billy borrowed a wagon and took his father home, but the knife had penetrated his kidneys, and three years later he died of complications related to the wound. During those years, the Codys would become part of the destruction that would come to be called "Bleeding Kansas." Their homestead was raided, the house burned, and the stock stolen. Billy's pony, Prince, a gift from his father on his fourth birthday, was brazenly stolen by a proslavery neighbor. The family lived on what wild game Billy could provide, until he found employment herding cattle for wagon trains and carrying messages from the lead wagon to the rear. At age eleven he drew a man's wages of forty dollars a month, all of which went home to his family. That same year, he killed his first Indian in a night attack, shooting a Mississippi Yeager rifle, a short muzzleloader, which he loaded with a ball and buckshot.

In the glare and blaze of the Wild West Show that Buffalo Bill Cody started in the 1870s, and in the hundreds of dime novels and magazine articles glorifying and mythologizing his exploits, the real adventures of the man have often been lost. Cody is sometimes seen as merely an actor with the world's greatest gift for self-promotion. It is true that, by 1900, he was the most recognized celebrity on earth. But in those packed years when he did ride on the American frontier, he was indeed an adventurer, a renowned buffalo hunter, a scout who never shirked a dangerous assignment (he won the Congressional Medal of Honor for heroism while serving as a scout for the Third Cavalry), an Indian fighter par excellence. And he did some of this while quaffing champagne with dukes over a dead buffalo, or just back to America from taking the Wild West Show before the Queen of England, or as was once the case, killing and scalping a Cheyenne subchief named Yellow Hand in one-on-one battle, while wearing what Cody historian Eric Sorg described in *Buffalo Bill: Myth and Reality* as "an elaborate velvet stage costume." The last incident occurred while Cody was acting as scout for Gen. George Crook, seeking the warriors who had just annihilated General Custer and his troops at the Little Bighorn. Cody would reenact the incident in his Wild West Show for some years to come, calling the scene, "The First Scalp for Custer," until he grew weary of it and dropped it from the show, perhaps because, as Sorg points out, he was conscious of acting out a very serious reality of death and scalping (Cody said that this was his first and only scalping), for the pleasure of audiences who could never understand what had really happened, or the context in which it occurred.

Such worries dogged him much of his life. Another man named Buffalo Bill, growing old in poverty in Topeka, Kansas, once wrote to him and said that he planned to confront Cody over the theft of his name if he brought the show to Topeka. Cody sent an employee to meet the man, and found that he had recently fallen on such hard times that he'd sold his treasured buffalo rifle. The employee found the gun, bought it, and returned it to the old hunter. Then he purchased the man's life story, in installments, to provide him with an income. There was no more dispute from him over the name.

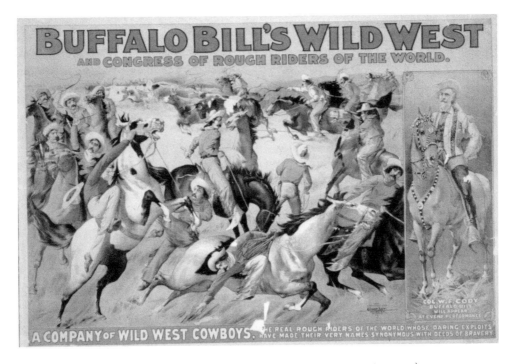

In the great age of the traveling show (the last decades of the nineteenth century) no spectacle was greater or more popular than Buffalo Bill Cody's Wild West Combination. At its height, the show had as many as 1,200 performers, including bands of Plains Indians led by Sitting Bull himself, Argentinean gauchos, Mongol horsemen, and the best markswoman of the age, Annie Oakley.
Library of Congress, LC-USZC4-1479

Although he ran the Wild West Show (it was first called The Buffalo Bill Combination, then Buffalo Bill's Wild West) for twenty years or more, at one time employing twelve hundred actors, he was never a skilled businessman. But as a showman, he had few equals. Fewer still could ever lay claim to employing such a bizarre pool of talent. Sitting Bull and twenty of his warriors appeared in the show. Wild Bill Hickok played himself for one year. Annie Oakley was the show's trick-shot champion. When the show expanded to include the "Congress of Rough Riders of the World," real Mongol horsemen played the role of Genghis Khan and his Golden Horde.

Cody's money flowed out as fast as it came in. He owned a vast ranch of eight thousand acres near Cody, Wyoming, and a dude ranch called Scout's Rest, in North Platte, Nebraska. The first was his retreat, and place for entertaining, which he did lavishly. The Scout's Rest became a kind of convalescent home for worn-out and injured performers from the Wild West Show. Contrary to the myth, Cody did not drink himself to death (until the very last years of his life he drank heavily, but it has been noted that he never missed a performance or a military assignment due to being drunk), and he did not die penniless, although his large fortune was worn very thin. In the tumult of business and the cutthroat profiteering of the day, he remained an innocent. He was among the first celebrities to advocate for the conservation of buffalo, and he spoke tirelessly on the wrongs done to the American Indians. He was also an early proponent of suffrage and the equality of women. Although the relationship was often stormy, he was married to his wife Louisa for almost fifty years.

Buffalo Bill Cody lived to be almost seventy-one years old. He died on January 10, 1917, in Denver, and despite his many requests to be buried in Cody, the town that he helped to found, he was buried in Golden, Colorado, at a lookout overlooking the Great Plains.

Annie Oakley provided a eulogy:

He was the kindest, simplest, most loyal man I ever knew. He was the staunchest friend. He was in fact the personification of those sturdy and loveable qualities that really made the West, and they were the final criterion of all men, East and West. Like all really great men he was not a fighter by preference. His relations with everyone he came in contact with were the most cordial and trusting of any man I ever knew . . . His heart never left the great West.

CHAPTER FOUR

Geronimo's Winchester Model 1876 Carbine

U.S. Army general George Crook was as tireless at advocating for the rights of Indians as he was at fighting and killing them. Crook called Geronimo, "the human tiger," and described him as one of the most formidable adversaries he had ever known in a life of warfare. Gen. Nelson A. Miles, exhausted by the Apache campaigns, simply said that Geronimo was "the worst Indian on earth."

There are canyons in the Sierra Madre of northern Mexico that are like passages to another world. The canyons twist upward from the deserts to elevations that catch cool breezes, rain, and snow. Cactus dwindles, giving way to oak and pine forests, springs and waterfalls, well-grassed plateaus where the Apaches, whose lives were spent in almost constant motion, kept small and temporary camps they called *rancherias*. From one of these passages, Skeleton Canyon, Geronimo led the last remnant of the Chiricahua Apaches, and the

The Winchester Model 1876 Carbine on display at the North American Indian Museum, Washington, D.C., was surrendered by Chiricahua Apache war leader Go-ya-thle, or Geronimo, to Gen. Nelson A. Miles, at Fort Bowie, Arizona, September 4, 1886.
Courtesy National Museum of the American Indian, Smithsonian Institution

last of his raiders, drawn from many different Apache bands, down onto the sun-blasted plains of Chihuahua, and headed north to final surrender to the Americans in Arizona. It was the first of September 1886. Decades of active and no-quarter warfare—a war that actually began with Apache raids against Spanish settlers in their country before the turn of the seventeenth century—was ending.

THE STORY OF THE WINCHESTER MODEL 1876 CARBINE

The origin of the Winchester Model 1876 Carbine owned and used by the Apache war leader Go-ya-thle, known as Geronimo, during his last years of raiding in the 1880s is unknown, though it could have been taken from any one of the hundreds of miners, stagecoach drivers and passengers, soldiers, scouts, and civilian ranchers and settlers killed by Geronimo's band during those years.

The Model 1876, often called the "Centennial Model" to celebrate America's first century, was produced in a standard model, a target model (available with the Vermier or Lyman aperture sights, wind gauge, and spirit level), and a carbine and a musket, both of which came with lugs to hold a bayonet. The Model 1876 was Winchester's answer to the call for a more powerful lever-action repeater than the Model 1866 and Model 1873, which came in Winchester .44 caliber rimfire and .44 caliber centerfire, respectively. Both calibers had served the manufacturer, and tens of thousands of shooters, very well, but they were underpowered for both warfare and big-game hunting, especially buffalo hunting, which reached a kind of frenzy during the 1870s as the last of the great herds fell to the market hunters. Buffalo hunting was still dominated by the very heavy, single-shot Sharps "Big 50" (.50–90), familiar in operation and a trusted brand to Civil War veterans, and, with its heavy cartridge extractor and simplicity, so utterly bombproof in the dust and blood and grease of commercial buffalo extirpation.

Winchester's answer was the Model 1876, in .40–60, .45–60, .45–75, and the mind-blowing .50–95, the last of which was purchased by African big-game hunters, and anyone else who could afford it, tote the heavy ammo, and stand up to the recoil. (Not surprisingly, the .50–95 was never a big seller, and examples are highly sought by collectors today.) The problem for the company to solve in designing the Model 1876 was how to develop a lever action that would handle the length of the bigger cartridges then available. The military, always scornful of the lever guns, had adopted the Springfield Model 1873, with its classic .45–70 round (also known as the .45–70–405, propelling a 405-grain chunk of lead), the first military breechloader. Winchester hoped to adapt their rifle to that cartridge. But the old toggle-link loading system of the Henry, the Model 1866 and Model 1873 could not be made to handle a cartridge of such extreme length. The answer was to develop a new cartridge, shorter, with a bottleneck to hold the bullet. The first to be produced was the .45–75 WCF (Winchester Center Fire) with a bullet of 350 grains. The "throw" of the lever to chamber that cartridge was still fairly long, but it was rendered reasonable by the much larger (than previous Winchester lever guns) size of the 1876s frame. The tubular magazine, mounted under the barrel, held eight of the powerful cartridges. Many sportsmen, including Theodore Roosevelt, preferred the smooth handling characteristics of the rifles produced with a half-magazine.

The Model 1876 was considered Winchester's state-of-the-art lever gun at the time, but buyers still complained about its accuracy (mostly due to the fragility of the sights) and its suitability for the abuse of warfare. It was not a big moneymaker for the company. As always with the lever guns, U.S. military sales never materialized. The Canadian Northwest Mounted Police purchased a batch of 1600 Model 1876 Carbines in .45–75. Despite many complaints from the Mounties about the durability of the weapons, they remained in service until 1914. Another mass buyer of the Model 1876, in the musket variation, was the Hawaii Territorial Guard.

President Theodore Roosevelt was one of the champions of the Model 1876, owning three of the rifles, two .40–60 carbines, and a .45–75. Hunting from his ranch near Medora, South Dakota, across the Great Plains to Yellowstone and beyond, Roosevelt wrote in *Hunting Tips of a Ranchman*: "It is by all odds the best weapon I have ever had, and I now use it almost exclusively, having killed every kind of game with it, from a grizzly bear to a big horn." In *An American Legend,* R. L. Winchester says, "The Winchester is the best gun for any game to be found in the United States. It is deadly accurate, as handy as any, stands very rough usage and is unapproachable for the rapidity of its fire and the facility with which it is loaded." Roosevelt's .40–60, a spectacular weapon with an engraving of a mountain sheep on its side plate, has been housed at the Gene Autry Western Heritage Museum. Perhaps the most beautiful Model 1876 ever produced was presented as a gift to U.S. Army General Phil Sheridan by lumberman W. E. Strong. In the big .50–95 caliber, with half-magazine, side panels inlaid with gold, engraved with Sheridan's name and scenes of the hunt, it is a lethal work of art.

The qualities of the more prosaic Model 1876s recommended them to more than just sportsmen. Granville Stuart, the Montana cattle baron and vigilante, rode the frozen winter trails of the state hunting down rustlers and other miscreants, Model 1876 at the ready. "King of the Cowboys" and general troublemaker in Tombstone, Arizona, Johnny Ringo owned one. Maj. Frank Wolcott and cattle detective W. H. Tabor carried Model 1876s during their ill-fated expedition to clean out rustlers in Wyoming's 1892 Johnson County War. Liver-Eatin' Johnson used one to "keep the peace" (a relative term when discussing Johnson's efforts) as a town marshal in Red Lodge, Montana, during the 1880s.

But it was the last of the great Indian raiders, Geronimo, who perhaps used the Model 1876 to its greatest effect in warfare.

CHIRICAHUA MOUNTAINS, SOUTHERN ARIZONA, MAY 1885

The horse was wrapped from neck to belly with the intestine of his herd mate, who, like a half-dozen others, had died of exhaustion at the hidden waterholes deep in the Chiricahua Mountains. The intestine sloshed with spring water as the horse clattered upward through the rocks, driven from behind by the lance of a mounted Apache warrior, the heat and white glare of the desert a malevolent force, powerful and crushing. The heat was the Apaches' friend, weakening the thousands of soldiers, American and Mexican, who rode in pursuit of them.

The warrior knew that his enemies could not match his people here, in their own country, as sheltering to the Apache as it was pitiless to the outsiders who would steal it from them. With him rode some of the most ferocious and hardened fighters the world has ever seen. Geronimo was leading. He was fifty-five years old and had never been a chief; he held no authority other than as a shaman in close touch with the *g'ans,* the mountain spirits who guided him. He had been a raider all his life, a man lit from within by the cold fire of fury stoked to a kind of madness by the murder of his first wife and children by Mexican troops in 1850. Geronimo followed the old Apache ways of war with a quiet religious intensity.

Beside Geronimo rode Nana, an old man of preternatural strength and wariness, already in his mid-seventies. Nana had escaped massacres, and taken part in them. He had lived on reservations and witnessed the fantastic treachery of the American invaders, and had listened to orders for the extermination of his people in both English and Spanish. As fierce as he was, some part of Nana seemed always to remain among his rancherias in the high Sierra Madre, in the company of the Apache children he loved, and who revered him as protector and grandfather. It was perhaps his love of his children and his country that made him such a terrifying force through almost sixty years of raids and warfare.

Naiche was the second son of the war chief Cochise. He had only recently joined Geronimo and the war trail, after years of trying to make peace with the Americans by settling on the reservations, enduring the starvation and sickness, the dust and heat of the wastelands where he and his people had been cast. After witnessing the murder of his prophet, the shaman No-ke-da Klinne, by American soldiers on the San Carlos reservation in 1881, Naiche recognized the futility of surrender and returned to Geronimo, and the war. Juh, Geronimo's cousin, and a revered leader of the Nednhi band of Apaches, came with him.

Lozen, a woman warrior about forty years old, was far in the lead of the band, scouting like a lethal wraith through the thorny scrub of sotol and ocotillo. The Apache did not always train girl children to be warriors, as they did boys, but any woman who desired the life of a warrior was welcome in their raids. Lozen was as respected as any male fighter. She was known to be in close touch with the g'ans, too, and since her early years, they had whispered to her the secrets of the Apaches' enemies, their numbers, their plans, their weaknesses and strengths. One of her great regrets was that she had been running from the soldiers, carrying the infant daughter of a friend to safety, when the Mexican troops had caught her people on the plains of Chihuahua, and massacred them at Tres Castillos. Many of her relatives and lifelong friends were among the seventy-eight women

Geronimo's band, from the oldest warrior to the youngest, were among the most feared fighters on earth. This photo was taken while they were still fugitives in their home terrain, one of the earth's most unforgiving places.
Library of Congress, LC-USZ62-46636

and children slaughtered, and among the fallen warriors were her brother, and one of the most respected, if volatile, of the Apache chiefs, Victorio. After the butchery was done, the remaining Apache children had been herded on foot to Chihuahua City, and sold as slaves (true to Apache form, many would escape and return to the mountains). The indestructible Nana had been one of the only survivors of the massacre. Lozen had ridden with him on his vengeance trail in the months that followed Tres Castillos, killing Mexicans—men, women, and children—over a huge arc of country. Even some Apaches would later speak of Nana's vengeance with horror in their voices.

Among the twenty or so fighters with Geronimo were a dozen *bronchos,* Apache raiders attached to no specific band, answering to no chief, as free

This photo was taken during Geronimo's last days of freedom; Geronimo and Naiche, the son of Cochise, on horses, Geronimo's son, Perico, with baby, March 27, 1886.
Library of Congress, LC-USZ62-46639

and merciless as lobo wolves. The bronchos, like any of the six established Apache tribes from whence they came, were mirrored in the country that formed them: to their children and among their own kind, they were kind, generous, and known for their humor and love of freedom, of their mild beer, tiswin, of dance and celebration. To invaders, of any stripe, they were utterly without mercy.

As the warriors sipped the rank water from the puckered mouth of the horse gut, the soldiers hunting them were becoming so dry that some of them were opening their own veins just to feel the moisture of the blood on their lips. Before the week was out, there would be plenty of blood, some of it theirs, soaking the desert sand across southern Arizona.

THE STORY OF GERONIMO

Go-ya-thle—"He Who Yawns"—was born about 1823, in the mountains of southern Arizona, somewhere near the headwaters of the Gila River. He was born during a time of war with the Mexican soldiers and people, and it is said that he took the Spanish name *Geronimo* from the cries of the victims of his raids, as they called out to St. Jerome for help. In 1850, near the settlement of Janos, in Chihuahua, Geronimo's first wife and three children were among many Apaches massacred by Mexican troops. From then on he fought the Mexicans, who had invaded Apache lands after defeating the other Indian tribes of Sonora, without regard for their status as combatants or settlers. The Apache considered themselves the first people of the region, and they reserved the right to raid all who dared in their ignorance or arrogance to try and settle in their country, or to dig its minerals, or to hunt its game. They were particularly disgusted by the mining operations that so obsessed the Mexicans and the Americans who came into their mountains, believing that such activity defiled the spirits of the place.

The massacre of Geronimo's family, while it was horrifying, was not a surprising event. Since 1837 the Mexican government, responding to the Apache's seasonal raids, and their attacks on mining expeditions in their country, had

Never a chief, Chiricahua Apache Go-ya-thle, or Geronimo, was a war shaman, and leader. General Crook, who knew him well, called him "the human tiger."

Library of Congress, LC-USZ62-36613

placed a bounty on Apache scalps: $100 for a man, $50 for a woman, $25 for a child. Such a policy, as might be imagined, led to atrocity, including the murder of innocent Mexican settlers and anyone who had long black hair. Not long after the bounty was established, two white men, James Johnson and his partner, a man named Gleason, proposed an entrepreneurial scheme to lure the Apaches to the copper mines of Santa Rita del Cobre under the pretext of giving a feast, then killing them all for their scalps. The plan worked almost too well. Johnson and Gleason, joined by a group of American trappers, set up a howitzer in the brush beside the feasting and drinking ground at the mines. The howitzer was loaded with nails, rocks, chains and other debris. When it fired, "It mowed a swath as clean as if a giant scythe had slashed through the heart of the crowd," according to Paul Wellman, in his 1935 book, *Death in the Desert*. Mexican soldiers whose task it was to guard the mine rushed forward to help the trappers kill the wounded. It is estimated that four hundred Apaches were killed in the blast and follow-up killings. The dead were scalped, their hair taken to Chihuahua City for the bounty. One Apache who escaped was Mangas Coloradas, a chief of what would come to be called the Warm Springs Apaches, a group that would eventually include Geronimo and his band. The vengeance that Mangas Coloradas and his Warm Springs band took upon the mines of Santa Rita del Cobre set the benchmark for the relentless violence of the next fifty years. The Apaches started with the American trappers in the Gila River Valley, killing twenty-four of them, burning them alive, or hanging them upside down over fires until their heads burst. They ambushed each pack train bringing supplies to the mines, staking the packers out on the sand for long afternoons of torture. No supplies reached the settlement of almost four hundred miners and their families. Johnson's band of trappers, camped near the mines, tried to escape north, and were struck, with Johnson being one of the only ones to escape. After many days, out of food, and in the grip of terror, three to four hundred of the miners and their families made a break for the plains, carrying whatever they thought they would need for the weeklong journey. The Apaches waited until they were well away from the settlement and begin to strike them at will. Only six are believed to have arrived at Janos, the small ranching town where Geronimo's family would be slaughtered, a dozen years later.

Mangas Coloradas would live a long, eventful life. He would make a tenuous peace treaty with the Americans during the Mexican-American War, allowing them to operate in his territory against the hated Mexicans. That treaty was broken when gold miners took advantage of the truce to invade; in 1851 a group of miners in the camp of Pinos Altos, Arizona, seized Mangas Coloradas as a kind of joke, bound him, and beat him with whips so severely that he carried the scars for life. It was this incident, and the hanging of the brothers of chief Cochise in 1861 by U.S. Army lieutenant George Bascom, that led to what has come to be known in U.S. history as "the Apache Wars." For the United States, embroiled in the Civil War, it was a bad time to break the peace with the Apaches.

During the Civil War years, Mangas Coloradas, Geronimo, Cochise, and other war leaders restored almost undisputed reign over their original lands, raiding at will; killing immigrants bound for the goldfields of California and stage passengers; driving cattle from ranches; taking prisoners, both American and Mexican (children young enough to learn the ways of the tribe, but old enough not to be a burden, were kept alive, and treated well enough that many survived and became Apaches); and sacking the forts and mines of the region. But there was a different future coming across the Great Plains. The Apaches began to feel the might of the new American military hardware being brought in from the raging conflict to the northeast: the howitzers, the exploding shells, the long-range rifles, and the coldly methodical tactics of troops who had seen some of the worst that war could offer. Extermination of Apaches became the order north of the border, just as it was in Mexico (Arizona still offered a $100 bounty on Apache scalps as late as 1866).

In 1863 Mangas Coloradas, then about seventy-five years old, was taken prisoner and murdered while meeting with the U.S. Army under a flag of truce. As the Civil War ended, the army, led by Gen. George Crook (whom the Apaches respected and called *Nantan Lupan,* the "Gray Wolf Chief") and a host of lesser officers were able to bring such might against the Apaches that most of them sought peace with the Americans. The result, at least for the first few years, was more chaos and suffering on both sides. American profiteers, stealing government-issued supplies, starved the Apaches who were trying to settle on reservations such as the San Carlos Agency, which offered some of Arizona's harshest desert, and where the Apaches felt they had been sent to die. Every Apache raid on white settlers in Arizona and New Mexico, at least some of which were made out of desperation by warriors whose families were starving, was used as an excuse by the Arizona profiteers to demand more soldiers and more military expeditions, which in turn ensured that there would be more supplies to sell and plunder in complex criminal schemes. Apache warriors like Geronimo and Naiche came to reservations and settled down, only to return to the war trail when conditions, the incomprehensible rules, and the constant threat of annihilation from Arizona citizens became too extreme. Still hoping to abide by American rules without starving, Geronimo and many other fighters disappeared into Mexico, and returned to the reservations in Arizona, laden with plunder from raids, driving herds of stolen Mexican cattle and horses. They were horrified when officers like General Crook confiscated and returned the herds.

Apache warriors from many bands, exhausted by both the terrible conditions on the reservations and the endless war with the Americans, decided that the best hope for the survival of their people was to help the Americans defeat the last of the Apache raiders. Now, famous army scouts like Tom Horn and Al Sieber were joined by Apache warriors, recognized as the only fighters on earth who might actually find and destroy Apache raiders in the desert and the mountains. The far horizon of the Apache Wars came into view. But between the soldiers and their Apache scouts, and that horizon, Geronimo and his hardened band rode, striking and raiding, seemingly at will.

THE LAST RAID

By early on a May afternoon, Geronimo and his fighters were leaving the Santa Cruz Valley of Arizona, ready to turn south into the fastnesses of Chihuahua's mountains, a long jagged line showing black against the white desert sky. Early in the day, they had struck the Peck Ranch. The cowboys had made a short stand; all of them were killed efficiently, with no casualties among the Apaches. The Peck family fared badly. Mr. Peck had been forced to watch the torture of his wife until he went thoroughly insane, after which the Apaches had set him free. His thirteen-year-old daughter was thrown across the withers of a horse ridden by a proud young warrior who, before the day was ended, would become an unnamed symbol of Apache courage and power.

Capt. H. H. Lawton, described by historians as "a desert athlete," was in pursuit, his soldiers and Apache scouts raising dust far behind Geronimo. The heliograph, the Army communication system of mirrors flashing Morse signals from the tops of mountain peaks, was in full flickering motion. The heliograph could carry a message though the roughest country in the southwest, eight hundred miles in four hours. Although Geronimo was little concerned by Lawton's pursuit, it did drive his band into a collision with seventy Mexican irregulars. The fighting was fast, unfocused. An Apache woman was killed, and in the melee the horse carrying the Peck girl and her Apache keeper was flattened by a bullet. The girl fought her way through the bullets and the dust and into the thorn brush and cactus. Against all odds, armed only with her own will, she escaped, eventually to rejoin her father (who recovered his sanity).

Her warrior keeper, afoot, watched as Geronimo's band disappeared, racing south. He ran uphill, rolling into the cover of the rocks. The Mexican irregulars, seventy of them, moved in for the kill, firing their weapons and trying to close with him. The Apache waited out the first hail of bullets. Then he began his own war. Over the course of a few minutes, he killed seven of the Mexicans, shooting each one once, in the head. Shooting and advancing upon the rest, he brought them to a halt, until terrified, they backed away. The young warrior then walked south, following his people into the desert.

His people had recovered from the short fight with the irregulars. In a canyon they came upon a half-dozen Mexican men working a small placer mine. They rode them down and killed them all. Farther south, seven more

In forty-two years of active duty as a soldier and officer, General Nelson A. Miles was in the thick of most of the major battles of the Civil War, was wounded four times, earned the Medal of Honor, and led the war against the Plains Indians. In 1886, he was sent to Arizona to conclude the long campaign against the Apache, and accepted the surrender of Geronimo and his last band of fighters.

Library of Congress, LC-DIG-cwpbh-00846

men, out cutting wood, looked up to see Geronimo's band riding fast upon them. When Lawton's soldiers came through the woodcutter's camp, all of the woodcutters were scattered in the terrible positions in which they had been killed.

On May 5, the U.S. Tenth Cavalry, riding into Sonora under an agreement with the Mexican government, discovered Geronimo and his people, including women and children, resting in a valley of the Pinito Mountains. The cavalry did not hesitate. The rush of horses and men was immediate, their rifles pouring fire into the Apaches, all of whom withdrew—but only for a second. The resting place that Geronimo had chosen was a natural ambush zone. From a huge semicircle of giant boulders above, the now-concealed Apaches returned the fire in what seemed to be coordinated volleys. Scorched, the troops fell back. The Apaches disappeared, and the cavalry, nursing their wounded, left them alone.

"... the general belief among the people is that extermination of the grown Indians and making slaves of the children is the only remedy."

But even the most relentless warriors must at some point find a sanctuary to rest, to feed themselves, their children, their horses. And in all of northern Mexico, in all the lost and empty mountain ranges of Arizona and New Mexico, there no longer seemed to be such a place. At the height of the pursuit, in the spring of 1886, Geronimo and his band of sixteen warriors, twelve women, and six children were the sole targets of five thousand American soldiers (one-fourth of the entire U.S. Army), five hundred Apache scouts, one hundred Navajo scouts, as many as three thousand Mexican soldiers, and a swarm of thousands of bounty hunters and militia.

Geronimo and his band surrendered on September 6, 1886. Geronimo presented his Winchester to Gen. Nelson A. Miles, a weapon of war wielded by one of the world's greatest warriors, the like of whom may never be seen on earth again. Geronimo's war was the last major uprising of Indians against the U.S. government.

For the Apaches, Geronimo and almost all of them, it was the end of war but not of suffering. They were rounded up, combatants and noncombatants alike, including most of the scouts who had served the U.S. Army with such loyalty during the campaigns, and shipped by train to Fort Marion, Florida, where they were interned as prisoners of war. A year later, they were removed to the Mount Vernon barracks complex in south Alabama, where tuberculosis and fevers killed almost a quarter of them. Eventually, faced with extinction from the hot and humid Alabama swampland, they would be allowed to travel west to Fort Sill, Oklahoma, where their former enemies, the Kiowa and the Comanche, offered them part of their reservation to live on. Geronimo died there, in 1909.

The story ends there, unless the reader wants to imagine that there are, in fact, canyons in Mexico's Sierra Madre that lead to other worlds, or at least to places unknown. A reader would have to admit, too, that the Apache mountain spirits, and those most closely allied with them, like Geronimo and Lozen, might know things that the rest of us, in this heavily settled, loud world that we have created from what we took from them, do not.

On April 10, 1930, a band of Apaches appeared out of the high mountains in Sonora, and attacked a settlement near the town of Nacori Chico. The raiders killed three people, loaded their horses with plunder, and disappeared back into the mountains.

CHAPTER FIVE

Joseph Smith's Ethan Allen Dragoon
Model Pepperbox Pistol

It was Carthage, Illinois, June 27, 1844, and the prisoners were in the debtor's cell, on the second floor of the jailhouse, more an apartment than a conventional cell. The windows were not barred, and they were open to the heat of the late afternoon. Outside, all was green, the heavy leaves on the white oaks trembled slightly, and there was a rumble of thunder from the west, where the clouds were building white and high above the verdant swamps of the river. The dishes from supper were washed and put away, pipes were lit, and the prisoners discussed the tribulations and dangers of the day that was passing. They had shared a drink of wine with their guards, but rather than lifting their spirits, it had made them sad and lethargic, longing for home and rest. Hyrum Smith, the Prophet's brother, stood at the window, and Brother John Taylor sang, a hymn in his low voice: "A poor wayfaring man of grief, hath often crossed me on my way, Who sued so humbly for relief, that I could never answer nay." Brother Willard Richards held his cane, a heavy length of hickory, as much a cudgel as a walking stick. These were times of utmost peril, and weapons, even for these men who trusted in the providence of the Lord first, were necessary. The Prophet, Joseph Smith, the most imperiled of them all, paced the floor, deep in thought, the handle of a six-barreled pepperbox pistol sticking out of his pocket. For a few minutes after five o'clock, in an afternoon that had been hot and noisy, with angry crowds seething, the sunstruck and humid town of Carthage seemed to be calming down. Against the odds, perhaps, the incarcerated men could live to see the cool twilight, and if that, perhaps, the dawn, when the Nauvoo Legion, an army of believers

An Ethan Allen six-barreled Pepperbox Pistol, Dragoon Model, .36 caliber, was used by Joseph Smith, founder and prophet of the Church of Jesus Christ of Latter-day Saints, when he was murdered by a mob in Carthage, Illinois, on June 27, 1844. This pistol was smuggled in to Smith by Cyrus Wheelock, while Smith was imprisoned in the Carthage Jail on charges of treason.

The silver plate on the grip is inscribed, JOSEPH SMITH HELD THIS WHEN MARTYRED JUNE 27TH 1844.

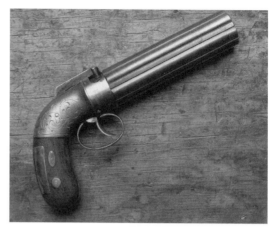

Image © by Intellectual Reserve, Inc., Courtesy of the Museum of Church History and Art

Carthage Jail
Courtesy of the Church History Library

three thousand strong, capable of striking down anyone who stood in the way, might arrive.

A volley of shots came from the street. For Hyrum, as he looked out the window, it was hard to understand exactly what he was seeing. A line of militiamen stood in front of the jail, their smoking weapons pointed up in the air. In front of them a crowd of men, their faces blackened like devils, all armed, rushed the front of the jail. The militiamen did not reload, did not lower their rifles and bayonets. Instead, some of them joined the blackface men in their assault on the jail. The doors crashed open, and the heavy thud of boots was on the stairs and in the hall. At first the attackers did not even try to open the cell door. They gathered before it, leveled their weapons and fired. Lead and pieces of wood exploded into the room. Some accounts say that Hyrum fired his own single-shot pistol through the door, in that last half second before the room became chaos. Whether he did or not, Hyrum was the first to die. A musket ball struck him in the face. "I am a dead man!" he cried out, his knees buckling. The door was slammed open, and a shower of bullets broke his leg, tore open his throat, smashed his skull.

The besieged prisoners tried to close the door against the strength of the determined assassins. Joseph stepped close to the jamb and fired his pepperbox out into the hall, jerking the trigger six times. Only the first three barrels fired, but there were yells from the close-packed mob of killers in the hall. Three of them were wounded. But it did not stop them. As the door was forced open again, John Taylor and Willard Richards attacked with their canes, slamming them down on guns and wrists that were forced through the gap, breaking hands and fingers. Pushed from behind, the mob burst into the room, shooting wildly. Taylor took a pistol ball in the leg as he leapt for the window; a sudden hail of fire came from outside, a bullet striking the watch in his coat pocket. The furious impact literally stood him up, silhouetted in the window, and he was struck twice more before he fell. Amazingly, he would survive, rolled under a bed, where a ricochet from the storm of lead would wound him yet again.

Joseph made it to the window. No one will ever know if he hesitated, caught between a rage of fire behind him in that room of devastating violence, and the streets of Carthage, alive with more enemies, all of them, it seemed, in crazed blackface, insane with hatred, and well armed with military weapons. The men in the doorway shot him first, two bullets to the back. In the whine and pock of musket balls coming from without, a single ball struck him in the chest. "Oh Lord, my God!" he said. He slumped forward and fell from the window, hitting the ground on his left side. The blackface killers took the stairs in leaps and bounds, racing to join the crowd that was gathering around the Prophet outside.

Willard Richards found himself alone in the shattered room. The door, in flying open, had pinned him in a corner and saved his life. Blood dripped from a minor bullet wound to his earlobe. He stepped over Hyrum, who had bled out on the floor, and stood in the terrible window. Richards would turn away before he witnessed what was next, and so the events are in dispute, but it is believed that the killers propped Joseph up against a curb and poured a final volley into him. It is said that a barefooted man was about to cut off Joseph's head with a bowie knife, but a sudden burst of strange sunlight falling on the death scene made him afraid. Richards, dragging the wounded Taylor to safety, heard a general hue and cry from the streets, "The Mormons are coming!" It was only a rumor, but it caught fire in the cooling and perhaps guilty hearts of the mob, and they ran, not waiting to seek out the survivors of their rampage. Taylor's ruined watch would be frozen forever at 5:16.24, marking the time of the outrage for generations of believers to follow.

Richards would bring the corpses of Joseph and Hyrum to Nauvoo. Ten thousand of their people were waiting there in grief and fury. Fears of a civil war were rife, but the Nauvoo Legion remained in the city, preparing to defend it, rather than going on the rampage that so many non-Mormon citizens feared. There would be some measure of vengeance taken, especially by the hard-as-nails wildman Orrin Porter Rockwell, the chief of the Danites, an armed group formed in part to protect the Mormons. But mostly there was just more unrest, and the preparations for the exodus to the West that would change the future of America.

A Mormon battalion
Courtesy of the Church History Library

THE STORY OF THE ETHAN ALLEN PEPPERBOX

The Ethan Allen or Allen & Thurber (Thurber was Allen's brother-in-law) Pepperbox represents a breakthrough in the ongoing search for portable firepower that drove so much innovation in pistol design during the mid-nineteenth century. The pistol carried by Smith was probably built from the 1837 Allen's patent. There was a race in the 1830s to see who could produce a reliable multishot handgun. The Darling Patent Rotary Pistol was patented in 1836, just before Sam Colt's 1836 single-barreled cylinder-loaded revolver changed the world of handguns forever. Ethan Allen was in the thick of design, and only a few months behind with his Model 1837 Pepperbox. All of these designs were percussion weapons.

The Pepperboxes were the handgun of choice for the '49ers, headed to the California Gold Rush, and were manufactured for almost thirty years, from 1835 through 1865. Others saw action in the Seminole Wars, the Mexican-American War of 1846, in the Indian wars, and as backup guns and hideout guns during the Civil War. All but a very few were smoothbore (the exception was a never-popular Robbins & Lawrence 1849 model), ranging in caliber from .28 to .36 or larger, and they came in a bewildering number of variations and manufacturers. An Allen patent on a design that rotated the barrels as the trigger was pulled—and it was a hard pull to make the weapon fire—made the pepperboxes the world's first double-action firearms. Early users recognized a weakness in the weapons: In a battle in close quarters, an assailant could easily grip the heavy group of barrels and render the weapon useless after a single shot. At least one manufacturer tried to solve this by making a twelve-barrel weapon, all the barrels encased in a smooth outer cylinder. Anyone grabbing that one would find themselves blown backward into eternity.

As smoothbores, with the hammer in the line of sight, and with the long trigger pull, pepperboxes were never accurate for more than a few feet anyway. From the beginning the Colt revolvers were the weapons of choice for men and women who lived in dangerous country where one's life depended on the ability to stop a man or animal attacker from a distance. The 1836 Colt Revolver could be viewed as a weapon capable of both offense and defense, while the pepperboxes were only for the latter. But a Colt cost $20 on the East Coast, right at the place of manufacture, and could sell for as high as $200 by the time it had been transported around the Horn or across Panama to the goldfields of California. An Allen Pepperbox carried a price tag of around $10, which is why the bulky and oddly balanced little weapon garnered an enviable share of the market. While it saw plenty of action in warfare and close-quarters battle under the open skies, it gained fame in the indoor world of the American West, as the easily concealed weapon for the businessman and gambler, the lawyer and carnival hand, the madam of rowdy brothels, and the lady traveling alone on dangerous streets. The pistol served Joseph Smith admirably in his last-ditch stand in the Carthage jail apartment, and would have served much better if the loads had been checked to ensure that they would all fire. Although it is believed now that only three barrels of the Allen actually fired, the author John Hay, who reported on the death of Smith in the *Atlantic Monthly* in 1869, wrote: "Joe Smith died bravely. He stood by the jamb of the door and fired four shots, bringing his man down every time. He shot an Irishman named Wills, who was in the affair from his congenital love of a brawl, in the arm; Gallagher, a Southerner from the Mississippi Bottom, in the face; Voorhees, a half-grown hobbledehoy from Bear Creek, in the shoulder; and another gentleman, whose name I will not mention, as he is prepared to prove an alibi, and besides stands six feet two in his moccasins."

THE STORY OF JOSEPH SMITH

The conflict that culminated in the murders of Joseph and Hyrum Smith at Carthage began with the Missouri Mormon War of 1838, when the Mormons were expelled from Missouri. According to historian Warren Jennings, the pioneers of the Latter-day Saints who had come to western Missouri to found their City of Zion had entered a kind of sociological hornet's nest. The Missouri land that the Saints viewed (through Joseph Smith's divine revelation) as both the Garden of Eden and their sacred inheritance was already well occupied by what Jennings calls "the apostles of individualism." In the early 1830s, when the Saints (many of them New England Yankees) first arrived in Missouri, the people they found living there, in scattered cabins and homesteads, were the parents and grandparents of Jesse and Frank James, Bloody Bill Anderson, William Quantrill, the Youngers, and a thousand other men and some women who would prove to be among the world's most brutal and effective guerilla fighters when the Civil War began, twenty years later. The Missourians were people who had abandoned Mississippi, Kentucky, and Tennessee as those places became settled, and they were not seeking to create a new community or be bound by any strictures of religion (or anything else) imposed by anyone other than themselves.

Joseph Smith was not exaggerating his perceptions of Missouri, when, according to his biographer Richard L. Bushman, he wrote, in 1831:

Joseph Smith Jr., founder of the Church of Latter-day Saints, or the
Mormon Church, was born December 23, 1805, and died June 27, 1844.
Library of Congress, LC-USZ62-123828

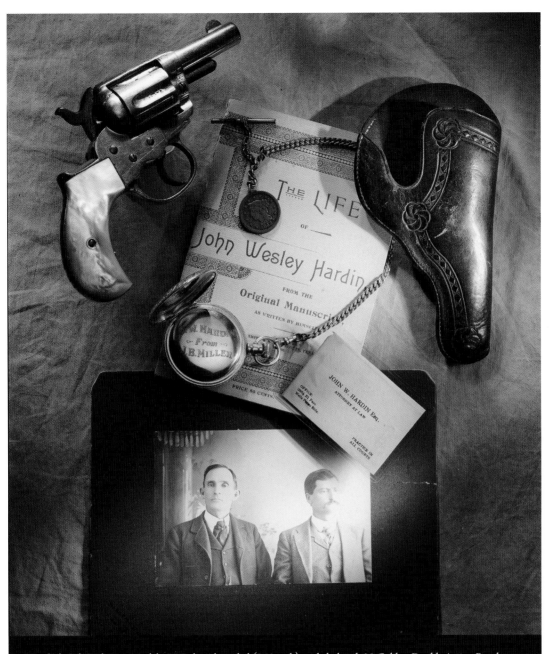

Hardin's Colt Lightning Model 1877, short barreled (2 ½ inch), nickel plated .38 Caliber Double Action Revolver, serial number 84304, was taken from John Wesley Hardin's body after he was shot to death by Constable John Selman, Sr. in the Acme Saloon, El Paso Texas, August 18, 1895. This revolver was given to Hardin as a gift and payment from James "Killin' Jim" Miller, and is inscribed on the grip "JBM to JWH." At the time of the gift, April of 1895, Hardin was practicing law in El Paso, and representing Miller in an attempted murder case against Sheriff Bud Frazer, with whom Miller had fought two gun battles resulting from a long-running personal feud. Frazer, a former Texas Ranger, had shot Miller multiple times in both fights, but Miller habitually wore a steel plate under his heavy dress coat, and survived with minor injuries. Hardin's attempt to prosecute Frazer on Miller's behalf failed. Miller resolved the issue in 1896 by blowing Frazer's head off with a double-barreled shotgun.

Texas gunfighter John Wesley Hardin's Colt Thunderer Model 1877 .41 Long Colt Double Action Revolver, serial number 73728, was confiscated from Hardin by Deputy Sheriff Will Ten Eyck in the Gem Saloon, on May 6, 1895, after a drunken Hardin used it to rob the Gem Saloon's crap

John Brown's custom Sharp's Model 1850, .44, was carried during the "Kansas Campaign," of 1856–1858, used in the Battle of Black Jack, the Battle of the Osawatomie, The Battle of the Spurs, and in many raids and skirmishes with pro-slavery militias between 1855 and 1858. Brown carried this gun in the infamous Pottawatomie Massacre of 1856.
COURTESY SMITHSONIAN INSTITUTE

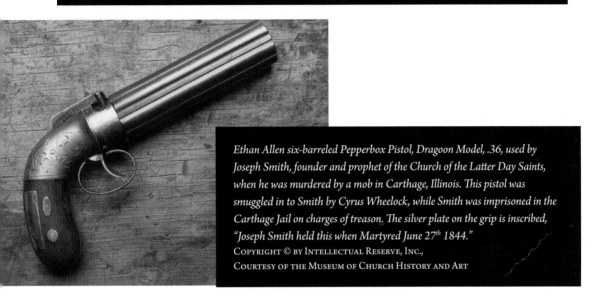

Ethan Allen six-barreled Pepperbox Pistol, Dragoon Model, .36, used by Joseph Smith, founder and prophet of the Church of the Latter Day Saints, when he was murdered by a mob in Carthage, Illinois. This pistol was smuggled in to Smith by Cyrus Wheelock, while Smith was imprisoned in the Carthage Jail on charges of treason. The silver plate on the grip is inscribed, "Joseph Smith held this when Martyred June 27th 1844."
COPYRIGHT © BY INTELLECTUAL RESERVE, INC.,
COURTESY OF THE MUSEUM OF CHURCH HISTORY AND ART

This Remington Model 8 .30 Caliber, Semi-Automatic, was presented to Texas Ranger Frank Hamer by the Remington Arms Company in 1922 and is currently exhibited in the Texas Ranger Museum, Waco, Texas. Hamer was the leader of the ambush that killed Bonnie Parker and Clyde Barrow; his Model 8's were known as "pear burners" because of his propensity for fierce rates of fire.
COURTESY OF SAM HOUSTON SANDERS CORPS OF CADETS CENTER, COLLEGE STATION, TEXAS

What Lucretia Borgia looked like in her prime, a 50-70 Springfield "Trapdoor" Model 1863, Second Allin Conversion, one of the great rifles of the West.
COURTESY BUFFALO BILL HISTORICAL SOCIETY, CODY, WYOMING

This is all that is left of the legendary "Lucretia Borgia," William "Buffalo Bill" Cody's personal buffalo rifle, 50-70 Springfield "Trapdoor" Model 1863, Second Allin Conversion, used in Indian fights and professional market hunting, and the rifle with which Cody won the name "Buffalo Bill."
COURTESY BUFFALO BILL HISTORICAL SOCIETY, CODY, WYOMING

This Winchester Model 1894, .30 Winchester Center Fire (known as the 30-30 Winchester) serial number 82667, was owned by Tom Horn, Army scout, interpreter, and fighter in the Apache Wars, man hunter for the Pinkerton Agency, and finally "cattle detective" in Wyoming and Colorado. Horn gave this rifle to Wyoming rancher Charles (C.B.) Irwin, three days before Horn was hanged at Cheyenne, Wyoming on November 20, 1903, for the sniping murder of fourteen-year-old Willie Nickel. The rifle was originally displayed at the National Cowboy Hall of Fame in Oklahoma City, Oklahoma, but is now believed to be back in the hands of the Irwin family.
COURTESY NATIONAL COWBOY & WESTERN HERITAGE MUSEUM

When Geronimo surrendered his Winchester Model 1876 Carbine to General Nelson A. Miles at Fort Bowie, Arizona, on September 4, 1886, he effectively ended the American Indian wars in the Southwest. The rifle is on display at the North American Indian Museum, Washington, D.C.
COURTESY NATIONAL MUSEUM OF THE AMERICAN INDIAN, SMITHSONIAN INSTITUTION

These beautiful Colt Model 1851's, Caliber .36, ivory handled, engraved at the Colt factory by master engraver Gustave Young, were the tools of the trade for one of America's most iconic western gunfighters. From the hyper-violent streets of Abilene, Kansas, to the last of the frontier in the Black Hills of South Dakota, the pistols shown here were Wild Bill Hickok's pride. They were in his belt (he didn't like holsters) when he was shot in the head and killed by Jack McCall in Deadwood, South Dakota, on August 2, 1876. They were sold for 25 cents apiece, along with Hickok's few other belongings, to help pay his burial expenses.
ON LOAN TO, AND ON DISPLAY AT, THE BUFFALO BILL HISTORICAL CENTER, CODY, WYOMING. SERIAL NUMBERS: 204672, AND 204685. ON LOAN TO BBHC FROM PRIVATE LENDERS.

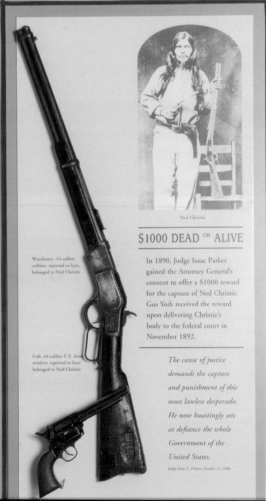

Ned Christie

$1000 DEAD OR ALIVE

In 1890, Judge Isaac Parker gained the Attorney General's consent to offer a $1000 reward for the capture of Ned Christie. Gus York received the reward upon delivering Christie's body to the federal court in November 1892.

The cause of justice demands the capture and punishment of this most lawless desperado. He now boastingly sets at defiance the whole Government of the United States.

Judge Isaac C. Parker, October 11, 1890

Winchester .44-caliber carbine, reported to have belonged to Ned Christie

Colt .44-caliber U.S. Army revolver, reported to have belonged to Ned Christie

Ned Christie's 1873 Winchester Rifle, Caliber .44 WCF (also known as the .44-40), is on display at the Fort Smith National Historic Site, Fort Smith, Arkansas. With this rifle, Ned Christie made history as a Cherokee warrior who would not surrender to what he considered the corrupt court of the white men, for a crime that he did not commit. For five and a half years he fought off numerous assaults by lawmen in the employ of the white courts. He never left the territory where he was born, dying in a climactic battle in 1892.
COURTESY MEMORIES BY JODY

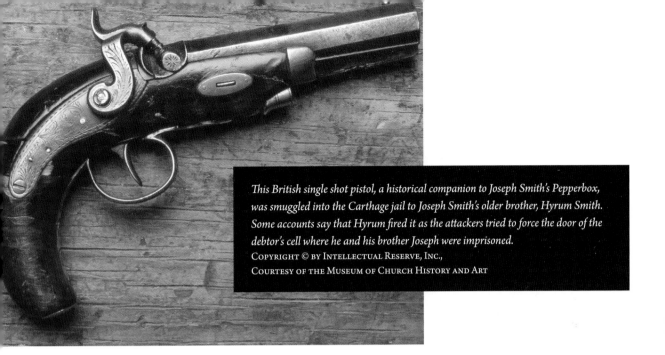

This British single shot pistol, a historical companion to Joseph Smith's Pepperbox, was smuggled into the Carthage jail to Joseph Smith's older brother, Hyrum Smith. Some accounts say that Hyrum fired it as the attackers tried to force the door of the debtor's cell where he and his brother Joseph were imprisoned.

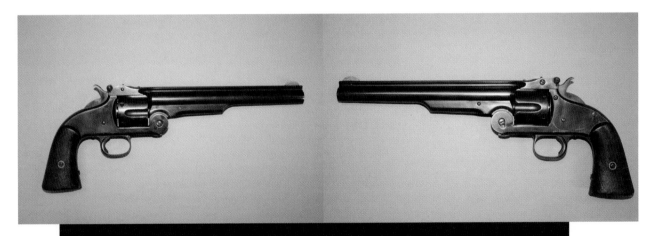

Smith and Wesson Model 3 American Revolver believed to be carried by Mexican revolutionary commander Doroteo Arango, also known as Pancho Villa, and used in the Mexican Revolution and the subsequent Mexican Civil War, conflicts that lasted from 1910 to 1920. This revolver is a single action, six shot weapon, caliber .44 Smith and Wesson, with an eight inch barrel. On display at the J. S. Adams Arms Museum, Claremore, Oklahoma. Purchased by Merle A. Gill from former "Villista" (a soldier in Villa's army) Pablo Gonzalez, in El Paso, Texas, in 1933. Gonzalez rode in Villa's Division of the North during the fighting in 1917.
COURTESY J. M. DAVIS ARMS AND HISTORICAL MUSEUM, CLAREMORE, OKLAHOMA

Colt Single Action Army Revolvers, Caliber .38-40, owned by lawman William Matthew "Uncle Billy" Tilghman, Jr. on display at the J. M. Davis Arms and Historical Museum, Claremont, Oklahoma. The Colt on the right, serial number 235639, was carried by Tilghman during part of his fifty-year career as a lawman.
COURTESY J. M. DAVIS ARMS AND HISTORICAL MUSEUM, CLAREMORE, OKLAHOMA

The Colt on the left also belonged to Tilghman. For many years this revolver was believed to have been a gift to Tilghman from Texas gunfighter John Wesley Hardin. However, curator Jason Schubert of the J.S. Adams Arms Museum, while conducting some unrelated research, discovered that the serial number of this revolver placed its manufacture in 1912, many years after Hardin was killed.
COURTESY J. M. DAVIS ARMS AND HISTORICAL MUSEUM, CLAREMORE, OKLAHOMA

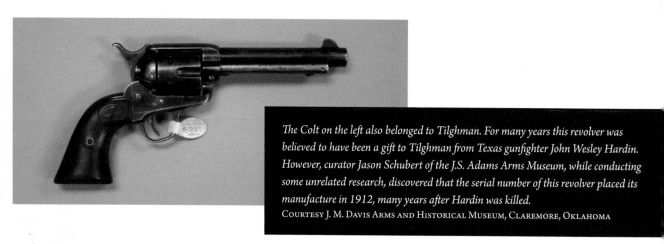

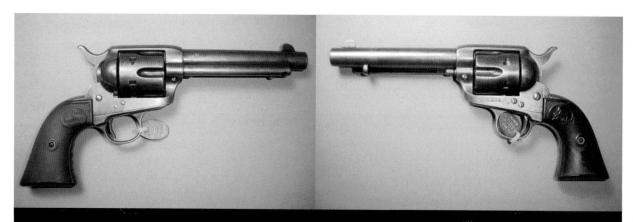

Tilghman was a U.S. Marshal, riding for the court at Ft. Smith, Arkansas, and the third member of "The Three Guardsmen" with Danish soldier of fortune Chris Madsen, and veteran Indian Territory lawman Heck Thomas. Tilghman helped to destroy the Bill Doolin Gang at that time, and, with Madsen and Thomas, brought in more than three hundred outlaws from the vast and lawless Indian Territories.
COURTESY J. M. DAVIS ARMS AND HISTORICAL MUSEUM, CLAREMORE, OKLAHOMA

Our reflections were great, coming as we had from a highly cultivated state of society in the east, and standing now upon the confines or western limits of the United States, and looking into the wilderness of those who sat in darkness; how natural it was to observe the degradations, lean[ness] of intellect, ferocity and jealousy of a people that were nearly a century behind the time.

The biography goes on to say Smith would soon find out, that, in regards to their ferocity at least, his earliest perceptions of the Missourians were correct.

Conflict came fast. By 1833 large numbers of Mormons entered the region near the river town of Independence, creating a real estate frenzy (a business dominated by Mormon settlers, who were, to what was probably an intimidating extent, hard working and entrepreneurial, the kind of newcomers who transform a region). Rumors circulated that the Mormons were abolitionists, and that they voted all in a block, making it certain that they would take control of local governments. Bands of Missourians began targeting Mormon homesteads and settlements. In Independence, the headquarters of the local Mormon newspaper, *Evening and Morning Star,* was attacked, the printing press destroyed. The local Mormon bishop and other Saints were tarred and feathered. Many of the Mormon newcomers did not have firearms and were easy targets. As the fighting worsened, the heavily armed Missourians favored strange face paints and bright shirts, like warring Indians, and these bizarre raiders rode, as many as five hundred at a time, under a red banner to symbolize blood. Mormon settlements were burned, their possessions stolen. The conflict would simmer until 1838, when it broke out into a small-scale war between Missourians and a band of armed Mormon men called the Danites, which had formed in reaction to the danger from Missourian attacks and, according to some Mormon dissenters, to enforce order in an increasingly divided community. Strife ruled the land, and during the early months of 1838, many acts of pillage and assault were committed by Missourian and Mormon alike. After a pitched battle between Missouri militiamen and Danites at Crooked River, Daviess County, Missouri governor Lilburn W. Boggs issued his infamous

Extermination Order: "The Mormons must be treated as enemies, and driven from the State if necessary for the public peace—their outrages are beyond all description." Missouri mobs took the order to heart. On October 30, 1838, a mob of 240 men descended upon the Mormon settlement at Haun's Mill and massacred nineteen people, including a ten-year-old boy.

At a standoff between Missouri militia—not a mob, but a force sent by the governor to restore order—and twenty-five hundred armed Mormon defenders, Joseph Smith and four of his leaders were seized while attempting to broker a truce. They were charged with treason for making war on legitimate militiamen at Crooked River, and sentenced to be executed. Realizing that such an execution would be both unjust and lead to bloody civil strife, some Missourians, perhaps directed by Governor Boggs, arranged to have their captives escape after some months of imprisonment. Most of the Saints—ten thousand men, women, and children—had already made a pell-mell exodus across the Mississippi River to Illinois, where they had been invited to settle. Everything they left behind in Missouri was either stolen or put to the torch.

On the banks of the river, on the Illinois side, they settled at a place called Commerce. No one mistook it for the Garden of Eden promised them in Missouri. It was swampland, and malaria, cholera, and typhoid descended upon the Saints like a series of biblical plagues. Nevertheless, the settlers went to work, building houses and gardens and digging drainage canals. When Joseph and his leaders escaped from captivity and joined the efforts, Joseph renamed the place Nauvoo. His followers often called it, "the city of Joseph."

> *"I am a rough stone. The sound of the hammer and chisel was never heard on me nor never will be. I desire the learning and wisdom of heaven alone."*
> —JOSEPH SMITH JR.

Nauvoo grew at an unbelievable pace, to become one of the largest cities in Illinois at the time. An impressive temple was constructed, a school system established. An influx of converts from Great Britain brought new ideas and new energies. But there were troubles. Early on, Joseph Smith held an

As depicted in this artist's rendition of the death of Joseph Smith, legend says that after Smith was murdered by members of the Carthage Grays, many of them in bizarre blackface and wigs, one of the killers was prevented from cutting off his head for a trophy by a strange light that came over the scene.
Library of Congress, LC-USZC4-4562

unprecedented amount of power in the city, as leader of the Church, head of the courts, commander of the militia now called the Nauvoo Legion, and mayor. As in Missouri, non-Mormon citizens of Illinois began to worry that his power, backed by so many newcomers, voting as a block, posed a threat to democracy. The citizens of the nearby cities of Warsaw and Carthage were astonished and threatened by the growth of Nauvoo, at the communalism, and at the religious beliefs of the Mormons. The concept of plural marriage was among the most controversial, even among the followers themselves. In the new city, 1842 was a year of ferment and tribulation. John C. Bennett, who had made a meteoric rise to power in the Church, was found to be having numerous affairs with women, married and unmarried, in the town, and defended himself by declaring falsely that "spiritual wifery" was a concept enjoyed and endorsed by Joseph Smith himself (plural marriage was sanctioned by the Church, but it was a formal marriage process, not at all what Bennett had been engaging in). Bennett, cast from power, became an enemy of Smith, and published an exposé of the alleged outrages of Smith and the Church. Growing numbers of anti-Mormon citizens paid close attention to the litany of immoralities that Bennett described.

Joseph Smith was still wanted for treason in Missouri. Whenever agents from Missouri crossed the river and arrested him, Smith would have the Nauvoo courts release him. There was a growing outcry in Illinois that this was more evidence of theocracy, and that the city, in the absence of legitimate law, was becoming a haven for criminality. Citizens of Carthage and Warsaw began to demand the expulsion of the Mormons from Illinois, and as in Missouri, militiamen declared themselves ready to force the issue, though the matter of the Nauvoo Legion, by 1844 a force numbering three thousand men, probably gave them pause.

In 1844 Joseph Smith announced his candidacy for president of the United States. That year, too, William Law, once a trusted friend of Smith's, a leader of the Church, and a prominent Nauvoo citizen, broke away and formed what he called the True Church of Jesus Christ of Latter Day Saints. Law was still a believer in Mormonism, but decried the corrupting influence of plural marriage on the Church, and the unhealthy blend of church and state in Nauvoo. He felt that as a prophet, Joseph Smith had failed. In a bitter contest Law started his own newspaper, the *Nauvoo Expositor*. The *Expositor*'s single issue condemned Smith's practice of polygamy seeking, Law wrote, "to explode the vicious principles of Joseph Smith, and those who practice the same abominations and whoredoms." It also addressed non-Mormon readers, assuring them that their rights would always be respected, and that no theocracy would be sought under Law's reformed church. That single issue of the *Expositor* fanned the anti-Mormon, or at least the anti-Smith, flames high, especially among those outside of the Church.

Smith led the city council of Nauvoo to declare the *Expositor* a public nuisance, citing its effect not on his reputation, but on its incitement of anti-Mormon sentiments, which were already on the verge of violence. The paper's printing press was destroyed by the town marshal on June 8, 1844.

Joseph Smith was charged by Illinois authorities with riot, related to the destruction of the press. After a tense couple of weeks, with the specter of civil war again stalking the countryside, Smith surrendered, to the fate that he knew was awaiting him in Carthage.

CHAPTER SIX
Chief Joseph's "Surrender Gun"—
Model 1866 Winchester Rifle

On Bear's Paw Battlefield, near Chinook, Montana, October 5, 1877, the Bear's Paw Mountains lay in a crescent to the south, shrouded in blowing clouds and snow. Chief Joseph and the last of his war leaders rode toward the soldiers slowly. Joseph's topknot was bound with a strip of otter hide, and his long braids hung down in front of his shoulders like heavy black ropes. Gen. O. O. Howard, the One-Armed Soldier Chief, and his officer, Col. Nelson Miles, whom the Indians called Bear Coat, waited in the wind and thin snow at the top of a rise. As the Indians narrowed the distance, small knots of soldiers gathered, themselves too exhausted and cold to be threatening. Some of these men would later claim that they could see the bullet holes, at least four of them, in Joseph's gray woolen shawl. His face and head bore raw stripes made by other bullets; his leggings and shirt were pierced by as many as a dozen more.

With a brass frame and receiver, the Model 1866 Winchester, lever-action carbine, came to be known as the "Yellowboy." This particular rifle, a .44 caliber Rimfire with a serial number of 102596 (indicating a manufacture date of 1872) belonged to the Nez Percé's Chief Joseph. It is currently housed at the Smithsonian's National Museum of the American Indian in Washington, D.C.
Courtesy National Museum of the American Indian, Smithsonian Institution

The warriors let Joseph ride the last few feet alone. He dismounted, a tall, stocky man of military bearing, and held out his rifle, a worn but well-cared-for Winchester Model 1866 lever action, a Yellowboy. Respectfully, General Howard held Joseph's gaze while an adjutant stepped forward and lifted the rifle from Joseph's hands, effectively finishing a war and putting an end to the freedom of the Nez Percé.

This rifle was used by one of America's greatest, if most reluctant, warrior chieftains, in a grueling contest of men and horses, gunpowder and steel. It took the lives of soldiers and, without doubt, saved the lives of women and children.

The seventy-five-day Nez Percé War cost the lives of 126 soldiers and officers, with another 140 wounded. The Battle of White Bird Canyon, early in the fight, was one of the army's worst defeats in the Indian wars, second only to Little Bighorn. Thirty-four U.S. Army cavalrymen were killed and two wounded. Two civilian volunteers were wounded.

By the day of surrender, the Nez Percé had lost 151 warriors, and had 88 more wounded. Thirty-six of their women and children had been killed, most of them in the attempted massacre by Colonel Gibbon and his troops and volunteers at the Battle of the Big Hole. The running fight carried Chief Joseph and his Nez Percé over 1,800 miles, east and north, as they were hoping to join forces with Sitting Bull in Canada. At the surrender the army took prisoner not only Nez Percé warriors but also more than four hundred women and children, many of them starving.

In 1860, when the first of the lever-action rifles appeared, a war between the states loomed like a gigantic thunderhead. The fighting between pro-slavery and abolitionist militias had already begun in Kansas and Missouri, a relentless and bloody tit for tat.

Just beyond the Kansas line, the Great Plains lay almost in freeze frame, a vast, open but dangerous passageway between the goldfields of California, the mines of Colorado and Montana, and the arable fields of Oregon. It was as if the plains were waiting for a different kind of violent storm to break upon them, a storm whose ferocity was only barely suggested by the first few wagon trains crossing them. Millions of buffalo and pronghorn sheep still migrated north and south with the seasons, attended by packs of lobo wolves. Elk, mule deer, and grizzlies roamed the river bottoms and the open prairies. The Blackfeet, Lakota, Comanche, and Cheyenne, to name but a few of the Plains Indian tribes, chased the buffalo, and raided far and wide, focusing on whites as well as each other, taking women, slaves, scalps, and horses. The posts of the United States Army, charged with protecting the main trails and the first few prairie settlers and miners, were manned by underpaid, ill-equipped, and badly trained troops who were deserting in droves (it was called "taking French leave"), preferring the promise of the goldfields or the anarchy of Denver or San Francisco.

America was in constant, and often hyperviolent, motion.

It was a very good time to be a gun maker.

THE HISTORY OF THE MODEL 1866 WINCHESTER

Benjamin Tyler Henry was a machinist at the Volcanic Arms Company in Norwich, Connecticut, far from the tumult of the western borderlands and the secessionist fury of the South. Henry and his fellow gun makers at Volcanic were working to solve one of the great weaponry challenges of the day: how to build a reliable and rugged repeating rifle with a cartridge to make it combat effective. They already had a serious loser in what was known as "the Volcanic" or the "rocket ball," a heavy lead bullet with a hollow base packed with black powder and a priming compound to set it off. It was unreliable, and it was notoriously underpowered. Nobody, least of all the ultracautious officers of the United States Army, were going to abandon their tried-and-true muzzle-loading Springfields (the Springfield Model 1861 would be the primary weapon of the Civil War, a muzzleloader that a skilled soldier could fire three times per minute, and one that made a fortune for the Springfield Company) for some weird "rocket ball."

For inspiration Henry looked closely at the then-new .22 short rimfire (a cartridge loved by every serious squirrel hunter, young and old, from the nineteenth century to the present). He also studied other prevailing revolver cartridges of the day, including, almost certainly, that used with the popular Colt .44 Dragoon. What he created was the .44 Rimfire, a self-contained metallic cartridge that could be loaded into a long tubular magazine and fed into the chamber of the rifle with a lever mechanism. The magazine and lever-feed system worked well, even if the cartridge itself remained on the short end of the power spectrum. Early trials with the rifle probably involved heavy—as large as 350-grain—bullets, seated on top of a charge of .40–60 grains of black powder. With that load, the bullet left the end of the 24-inch barrel at a slothlike 750 feet per second. Fine tuning brought the bullet weight and the charge down. Twenty-five grains of powder behind a 208–210 grain bullet would push the bullet at almost 1,100 feet per second and deliver at least 540 pounds of energy to its target. It wasn't modern performance, even for 1860, but it would kill you.

Most importantly, it could do it sixteen times without reloading. The Henry Rifle, produced by the New Haven Arms Company in 1860, was probably the first firearm to be described as "the rifle you load on Sunday and shoot all week." Firing wildly, and levering fast, a good hand with the Henry could shoot the weapon dry in twelve seconds. Aimed fire could empty the rifle's magazine in under a minute, a terrible barrage to face as one struggled to tamp down a muzzleloader or draw a wishful long-range bead with a pistol. (There was one serious design flaw—the rifle lacked a foregrip, and under rapid fire the barrel and loading tube got so hot that you couldn't hold onto it.)

Yes, the best pistoleers of the day could shoot fast with the Colt Navy .36 revolvers, too, but nobody could deny that a new era in weaponry was dawning. The Henry displayed the beauty of form and balance and handling ability that would make the lever guns popular for more than a century to come. It *felt* right, and compared with the pistols it offered the fantastic accuracy of a long gun. The sun was rising on a brief and explosive golden age of close-range small arms combat, high-speed deadly clashes at what the old timers called "waltzing distance." The Henry .44 Rimfire, with its colorful brass frame and receiver, was the star of the day.

As the storm of war broke upon the nation in 1861, production of the Henry was still in its infancy. The rifle never found great currency among the rank-and-file soldiers of the conflict—their leaders considered the lever-action mechanism too delicate for rough combat, and they knew that a terrified soldier facing a charge with a repeater would be more likely to waste expensive bullets with rapid shooting. The armies stuck with the reliable Springfield muzzleloaders, purchasing only about 1,700 of the Henrys for special units and for some elite troops in infantry companies such as the Twenty-third Illinois. Of the fourteen thousand Henrys produced between 1860 and 1866, many were purchased for use as personal arms by soldiers and militiamen from Missouri to Indiana, and there is no doubt that the rapid staccato wham! wham! wham! of the little .44 could be distinguished in many a battle amidst the roar of massed musket fire and the scream of shrapnel. And it was increasingly heard farther west in running engagements from Kansas to Mexico and California.

For the Plains Indians, the world's greatest aficionados of beautiful weaponry, to own a Henry was a dream; to face it in battle, perhaps, a nightmare.

Benjamin Tyler Henry would not be led to wealth by his revolutionary creation. For one thing the rugged Spencer Repeater would enter the market right after the Henry, and provide stiff competition for his less-powerful and more delicate lever gun. And when the Civil War ended in 1865, the nation was awash in guns of every description, sold by the piece and by the crate or wagonload. The Henry might have been vastly superior, but many other weapons were more affordable and available.

After Henry went bankrupt in 1866, he was hired by Oliver Winchester, a Connecticut businessman with an interest in everything from textiles to weapons design. Henry would work as a foreman at the new Winchester Repeating Arms Company, ultimately helping produce the Model 1866 Winchester "Yellowboy," destined to be among the dominant guns of the western frontier. Henry's patented toggle-link lever system remained the same, but the magazine tube was extended to hold seventeen rounds, fully enclosed to keep out debris, and equipped with a strong spring to feed cartridges back to the lever. It had a spring-steel loading gate in the receiver of the rifle (a fantastic step forward in battle ergonomics) as well as a wooden foregrip, ending the era of scorched fingers and refining the weapon's balance and control. It came in either a twenty- or twenty-four-inch barrel, the short-barrel model sacrificing three rounds of capacity in the magazine. In the thirty-two years (1866–1898) that the rifle was in production, 160,000 of them went forth into the world. Because of their beauty and color, they were extremely popular with Native Americans of almost every tribe, who often decorated them lavishly. A warrior might etch a cross into the steel to represent the four directions, create a sunburst on the stock with brass tacks, or carve a silhouette of a buffalo into the wood. For white men the weapons were primarily tools, but for the Indians they seemed to represent something far more profound, an extension of the power of self, a connection to the worlds of living, fighting, and dying.

THE STORY OF CHIEF JOSEPH

When and where Chief Joseph acquired his Model 1866 is a mystery now, the answer lost in the mists of time and death, as lost as the warriors Yellow Wolf, Toohoolhoolzote, White Bird, and Joseph himself. If Joseph owned it when he was living in his ancestral homeland of Oregon's Wallowa Valley, it was still only a hunting rifle, not yet a weapon of war.

Today, the Wallowa Valley is still a relatively quiet and rural place, with a growing emphasis on tourism and sightseeing. But of the many travelers who come to the valley for the fly-fishing, rafting, or shopping, few are aware of the tragic events that took place here less than 150 years ago. If the ghosts of Nez Percé men, women, and children whisper on the stream banks or drift quiet among the ponderosa pines, few people see or hear them.

Late one night in August of 1871, a breeze from the Eagle Cap wilderness blew across the confluence of the Lostine and Wallowa Rivers, ringing a bell above the grave of Old Joseph. A man who had worked for years to make peace with the white settlers who were swarming into his ancestral lands, Old Joseph had died just that day. He'd been buried, not in the fashion of the

Heinmot Tooyalaket, or Thunder Rolling in the Mountains, was known to the white people as Chief Joseph of the Nez Percé.

Library of Congress, LC-USZ61-2085

Christians or even in the traditional way of the Nez Percé, but in the new way of the Dreamers, a faith that would play a major role in the wars to come.

The chieftainship of the Nez Percé passed to his son, *Heinmot Tooyalaket,* meaning "Thunder Rolling in the Mountains." He was known to the whites as Young Joseph. The new chief was thirty-one years old and had a six-year-old daughter. It was often remarked by white men and Nez Percé alike that Young Joseph had the natural demeanor of a chief, a calm reserve and a respectful way of speaking that instilled trust in anyone who dealt with him. Although he was a tall, strong man, he left the hunting and war party leadership to others, concentrating instead on the larger issues brought about by white settlement. He believed he could lead his band along a kind of razor's edge between resistance and accommodation.

He was wrong.

BEGINNING OF THE STRUGGLE

By the mid-1860s surveyors had come into the Wallowa Valley and divided the Nez Percé's land into standard 640-acre sections, preparing it for settlement by whites.

The tribe, always a loose collection of bands in which chiefs had only as much authority as the people granted them, had been further divided in 1863 when some bands decided to sell their rights to the Wallowa Valley and most of the rest of their claimed territory. These bands had also embraced Christianity, cementing their peaceful intentions with the white settlers. But Old Joseph refused to sign what he called the "thief treaty" and also rejected the Christianity that he felt was weakening his people and making them stooges for the whites.

He and his band of "non-treaty Nez Percé," including his brother Ollo-kut, and his son Young Joseph, had found another faith, that of the Dreamers, based on the teachings of the hunchbacked prophet named Smohalla, a shaman of the Wampanum tribe. Smohalla became an itinerant prophet, wandering among the tribes of the Columbia River headwaters and demonstrating a complex ritual that he said would reawaken the old spirits that the Indians had neglected in their star-struck embrace of white customs. The Dreamers, as can be seen in photos of Joseph and Ollokut, wore their hair in a high wave in the front and carried various charms and symbols related to their faith. And they could not sell land, ever. As quoted by Dee Brown in his classic, *Bury My Heart at Wounded Knee,* Joseph said: "The earth was created with the assistance of the sun and it should be left as it was . . . the country was made without lines of demarcation and it is no man's business to divide it . . . I claim a right to live on my land, and accord you the privilege to live on yours."

In 1873 Chief Joseph petitioned President Ulysses S. Grant to allow his people to remain forever in the Wallowa Valley. Grant, recognizing the long friendship between the Nez Percé and the American citizenry, issued an executive order to remove the valley from any plans for white settlement. Pressure immediately began to mount to rescind the order. In a move that may have been prompted by a campaign of deliberate misinformation, President Grant rescinded his order, and reopened the Wallowa Valley in 1875. The Nez Percé stayed in the valley, but trouble came on fast. Squabbles broke out over grazing rights, with settlers stealing Nez Percé horses and branding them, making it impossible for the Indians to recover them. A scuffle over more horses led to the shooting death of a young Nez Percé man named Wilhautyah. Oregon's governor Lafayette Grover demanded that Joseph's non-treaty Nez Percé be removed to the tiny reservation in Idaho where the Christian members of the tribe had settled.

Gen. Oliver Otis Howard, a one-armed Union veteran of almost every major battle of the Civil War, was the officer chosen to remove Joseph and his people from the Wallowa. Howard did not relish the job, and privately said that Joseph and his people should be left alone. But as a career military officer, there was never any doubt that he would carry out his orders. In May 1877 Howard called a conference with Joseph and his leaders at Lapwai, about ten miles east of modern-day Lewiston, to announce the removal plans. Joseph rode there with White Bird, Looking Glass, Ollokut, and Toohoolhoolzote, the Dreamer shaman of their band. Oddly, like Smohalla, Toohoolhoolzote was renowned for both his ugliness and his eloquence in speech.

At Lapwai, Toohoolhoolzote argued fiercely that no one had the right to remove his people; that they had signed no treaty; and that the earth could not be divided, bought, or sold. There was, logically, no way for Howard to argue with him. All questions of the Dreamer or any other religion aside, the Nez Percé had lived on the land for some centuries, had not sold it, and it was now being taken from them by force and given to white settlers.

Howard did not try to argue for long. He had Toohoolhoolzote arrested, and then announced that the non-treaty Nez Percé would move to the reservation in Idaho within thirty days or face attack by the army.

Joseph responded that there was no way they could collect all their livestock in such a short time. The Snake River was running wild with snowmelt. Howard repeated his order, adding that if the army was forced to drive the Indians to the reservation, any livestock left outside its boundaries would become the property of the white settlers. Toohoohoolzote was released, and Joseph and his men rode west to the Wallowa. It is recorded that Joseph continued to argue against war or retaliation, and even suggested that he would give up his claim to the Wallowa to avoid war or bloodshed. Looking Glass, who was the only one of the leaders with extensive experience in battle (he and his band had spent time in Montana where they had fought with the Crow against the Sioux), seemed to agree with Joseph.

But when they arrived in the Wallowa, events and emotions were running as fast and high as the Snake River. The soldiers were already there. In her exhaustive book, *The Saga of Chief Joseph,* historian Helen R. Howard describes the tense scene, "We held a council," Joseph said, "and decided to move immediately to avoid bloodshed." Toohoohoolzote, outraged by his imprisonment, argued for war. He declared that blood alone would wash out the disgrace General Howard had put upon him. White Bird, one of the oldest chiefs, and with fifty warriors in his band, had quietly assured his fellow chiefs for years that war against the whites was the only honorable option. "It required a strong heart to stand up against such talk, but I urged my people to be quiet, and not begin a war. I said in my heart that, rather than have war, I would give up my country. I would give up my father's grave. I would give up everything rather than have the blood of white men upon the hands of my people." ("An Indian's View of Indian Affairs" *North American Review,* April 1879, Joseph, quoted in *The Saga of Chief Joseph,* by Helen A. Howard). Joseph prodded the reluctant band to leave the valley and head east, a journey that would turn out to be both an epic of human endurance as well as an epic of inhumanity. The young men at first defied his orders to leave, but later followed him, helping ferry the women and children across the raging Snake River in bull boats made from buffalo hide. It was a dangerous crossing, with no human lives lost. But a late spring thunderstorm was pounding down, swelling the already-flooded river. When it came time to drive the livestock across, the current was too much. Many of the horses and cattle fought the icy river to exhaustion, and disappeared beneath the roiling surface. The rest of the herd stalled on the Oregon side of the river, guarded by a few distracted Indians, but soon to be stolen by a party of white men.

Joseph's band made it across the Salmon River to join White Bird's people at a place called Rocky Canyon, where they held a conference. Never before had the Dreamer shamans spoken with such eloquence or such fury. The camp seethed with the desire for vengeance. It was believed that the army might already be on its way to attack them. Joseph and Looking Glass endured taunts and insults for their stand against violence. In the end the issue was decided by a young Nez Percé man from White Bird's band named Walaitits, whose father had been murdered by a settler. The murderer, Larry Ott, had suffered no penalty for the killing. On the tenth night of the conference, Walaitits and his friends rode away toward the Salmon River country, which was well populated by settlers and miners. At some point they found liquor, which stoked the fires.

Larry Ott was long gone from that country, but the warriors killed three men that first night, taking horses and guns in the raids. The raiding continued the next night as the warriors killed and wounded men and women and children. The plunder they took was used to buy more guns and ammunition in towns that had not yet heard of the killings. As the marauding continued, more whites would be killed and wounded and the atrocities would escalate. A little boy was captured and stomped to death; a young girl was stabbed in the neck and had part of her tongue cut off. It was still only a handful of young Nez Percé men taking part, including apparently Toohoolhoolzote, who was said to have joined the raiders with his own small band. Whiskey trader Samuel Benedict, who had killed an Indian in 1875 without repercussions, was shot and wounded. Richard Divine was killed, and a man, Harry Mason, who had recently beaten two Indians with a whip was chased down and killed.

There could be no more talk of peace. The gallows awaited Joseph as surely as they awaited White Bird or Walaitits. The destruction of the people was almost assured. There was no reason not to fight.

For Toohoolhoolzote, the war had already begun. He led his band to a camp at the mouth of White Bird Canyon. Scouts monitored the movements

For decades after the Nez Percé War ended, there was debate about which Indian leader was responsible for their brilliant tactics. Perhaps Looking Glass, the veteran horse-warrior of the buffalo country, was responsible. Or maybe Joseph, possessed of so many unique powers, was unique in his understanding of war as well. And a warrior named Mox. Mox seemed to have a genius for keeping the horse herds protected and for moving women and children out of harm's way. It is a measure of the chiefs that none who survived the campaign ever claimed to be the war leader. Joseph himself never related any of his exploits except for those in the final battle. What is most remarkable, and most probably true, is the thesis put forth by Helen Addison Howard in her book, *The Saga of Chief Joseph.* "The whites have invested him (Joseph) with the title of military genius, a quality shared, the Indians avow, by many warriors and chiefs of the five bands." And Chief Joseph himself, when asked how he and his chiefs had learned such advanced military strategy, said simply, "The Great Spirit puts it in the heart and head of man to know how to defend himself."

of the soldiers, setting fire to haystacks to mark their approach. After night-fall the scouts called out with coyote howls. In a camp about a mile away, Joseph's wife was giving birth to his second child, a girl. On the morning of June 17, the soldiers entered the valley below the mouth of the canyon. Many Nez Percé warriors, including Walaitits and the young men from the raiding parties, were already in position to fight. Even as the soldiers rode toward them, in this long, last, wide-eyed moment, Joseph hoped to avoid this fight. He sent a party of Indians forth under a white flag, hoping that the soldiers had brought a Nez Percé who could interpret and help explain that the kill-ings had been perpetrated by a small group of the tribe's warriors. But that hope was dashed, too, as Arthur Chapman, an interpreter for the soldiers, saw two Nez Percé horsemen riding to take the high ground far beyond the truce party. Chapman raised his rifle and fired at them. A warrior hidden in the rocks returned his fire. A flurry of shooting began, and the Indians, after an initial charge by young men, withdrew silently, pulling the soldiers and their civilian volunteers deep into a perfect series of ambushes, with text-book fields of fire and cross fire. Although a warrior named Three Eagles said later that his band had had only fifty rifles at the start of the Battle of White Bird Canyon, and were mostly armed with bows made from syringa wood, or the short and powerful "horn bows" made from the boss of a bighorn sheep's horn, the soldiers reported that the Indian snipers perched above them were firing high-capacity Winchesters, producing a withering barrage of bullets. Among the soldiers killed were Lt. Edward Theller and all eighteen of his men, who were caught in a box canyon and annihilated. At the end of the battle, thirty-four soldiers lay dead. The Nez Percé, who suffered only three wounded, retrieved sixty-three rifles and uncounted pistols from the fallen and panicked soldiers.

Looking Glass and his large band had not taken part in the battle of White Bird Canyon, proceeding instead to the reservation. They were neu-tral in the conflict so far. But Howard was unsure of this fact (some of the young men of the band may have taken part in the battle without Look-ing Glass's knowledge), and he sent troops under Capt. Stephen Whipple to arrest Looking Glass and his leaders. As Whipple and one of Looking Glass's leaders were discussing the terms of surrender, "Dutch" Holmes, a local volunteer with the troops, decided to settle an old grudge, and fired his rifle into the camp. In the fight that followed a Nez Percé child was killed, as were Lt. Sevier M. Rains and his ten men, who galloped into an ambush. About a month later, Looking Glass and his band had joined with Joseph in time for the Battle of the Clearwater. There were now about three hundred well-armed warriors and about four-hundred-and-fifty women, children, and aged, plus hundreds of horses and cattle. The chiefs made the only decision available to them: They would go east and join forces with Sitting Bull in Canada.

The running war was on.

THE RUNNING WAR

On July 11, at what would be known as the Battle of the Clearwater, the army attacked the Nez Percé with an artillery barrage, and heavy fire from Gatling guns. But the steep canyon country favored the tactics of the Indians, who, instead of taking flight, assaulted and counterassaulted the dismounted troops. Soldiers reported that this was the first battle in history in which Indians used siege tactics and entrenched positions. The battle was a deadly and exhausting chess game, carried on over a distance of twenty miles. On July 12, Howard and two of his best commanders used a technique that Howard called "rolling up the enemy's line," a feint in one direction, then a quick about-face turn to charge. It worked, and broke the deadlock between the forces. But the army was too mauled to apply a coup de grâce. As Lt. William Parnell would write of the Nez Percé, "their retreat to Kamiah was masterly, deliberate and unmolested, leaving us with victory barren of results."

The next major fight was at the Battle of the Big Hole, on August 9. General Howard used a modern invention—the telegraph—to command Col. John Gibbon to attack the Nez Percé, who believing themselves far ahead of pursuit were resting at a camp beside Montana's Upper Big Hole River.

Gibbon and his troops, aided by a squad of civilian volunteers, attacked at first light, and completely surprised the sleeping camp, pouring volleys of fire into the tipis, causing destruction among the women and children. The attack was a rout, throwing the Indians into wild confusion. Accounts of the battle are rich with horror, of children smashed by bullets and boot heels, of vicious hand-to-hand battles in the freezing river waters and dark sloughs, and in the almost impenetrable willow thickets along their banks. But the Nez Percé rallied quickly. White Bird rode among the warriors, exhorting them to recover their valor and avenge their dead, a call that was answered even by women and children, some of whom had taken up the weapons left behind by their men in the terrible first moments of the attack. The marksmanship of the Indians had never been better, their tactics, even in their disarray, seemed flawless. Gibbon's men, and the volunteers, were decimated. The howitzer that they had so painstakingly dragged into the wilderness was overrun and lost (though the Nez Percé were too unfamiliar with it to fire it). Pinned down, Gibbon and his remnant force would have been annihilated save for the pell-mell race by General Howard and a powerful force to rescue them. Howard found Colonel Gibbon wounded in the legs, his commanding officers were mostly dead, part of a gruesome tally of thirty-one dead and thirty-eight wounded.

The Nez Percé gathered what they could of their people, horses, and belongings, and raced southeast, running again. They left a fearsome array of dead behind: at least eighty of their people, twelve warriors, and the rest women and children. Joseph would later say that 208 of his people died as a result of the terrible day at the Big Hole River, many of them dying of their wounds on the flight south, across Targhee Pass and into Yellowstone National Park, fighting rearguard, and straight-on battles almost the entire way. Once inside the newly created Yellowstone National Park, the Nez Percé would make further history by capturing (and killing some of) the first two parties of tourists ever to try and enjoy the natural wonders there. From tourists to telegraphs, howitzers to Gatling guns, from syringa bows to Joseph's Model 1866 Winchester, the Nez Percé were at war in a vast gulf between ages, in the swirl and dust and flux of explosive change.

As such, perhaps fate could not have treated them otherwise. The first week of October found the Nez Percé along Snake Creek on the flank of the strange Bear's Paw Mountains, an "island range" of rounded peaks that stands on the prairie like a heap of stones, black with lodgepole pine, the only timber for miles around. The Indians had found a small remnant herd of buffalo, and had killed some of them and eaten well, probably for the first time in weeks. They were less than fifty miles from Canada, less than fifty miles from the camps of Sitting Bull, with his two thousand seasoned warriors fresh from their victory over Custer.

Rimfire Cartridge

In 1934 the Winchester Company discontinued the .44 Rimfire cartridge. With it was laid to rest an entire era of American history. During the life of the .44 Rimfire, the Union had been preserved at terrible cost—more than six hundred thousand dead among the combatants, North and South. What had been one of the world's most impressive assemblages of wildlife, the buffalo and the rest of the plains game herds, were exterminated but for remnants. By the time the cartridge was discontinued the Indians, the former rulers of the Plains, were at perhaps the lowest level of their population, confined and defeated. Would-be settlers were fleeing their homesteads on the prairies by the tens of thousands (in Phillips County, Montana, during the 1920s, homesteaders would leave in such haste that six thousand head of horses would be left abandoned and drifting on landscape devastated by plowing, grazing, and drought). 1934 was the dirtiest year of the "dirty thirties," the highpoint of the American Dustbowl. In plowed fields and cutbanks across the West, the old metallic cartridges, with the distinctive H stamp on the heads, can still be found, relics of an era of explosive change.

SURRENDER OF CHIEF JOSEPH AND HIS PRINCIPAL WARRIORS AT GENERAL MILES'S HEADQUARTERS, OCTOBER 5–6.
MONTANA.—THE NEZ PERCES WAR—INCIDENTS IN THE DEFEAT AND CAPTURE OF CHIEF JOSEPH BY GENERAL NELSON A. MILES.
FROM SKETCHES BY G. M. HOLLAND.—SEE PAGE 139.

On the occasion of his surrender to General Nelson A. Miles, at the Bear's Paw Battlefield in Montana, Chief Joseph is famously supposed to have said, ". . . Hear me, my chiefs, I am tired. My heart is sick and sad. From where the sun now stands, I will fight no more forever."
Library of Congress, LC-USZ62-129681

While Nez Percé horsemen were chasing buffalo on October 5, a detachment of Cheyenne scouts had been watching them, and reported their presence to Bear Coat Miles. Howard was coming, too, from the Missouri River, in hot pursuit. Miles began his charge upon the Nez Percé from half a mile away across the grassland, a thundering wall of warhorses and cavalrymen. The charge was dramatic, but a mistake. At two hundred yards the Nez Percé warriors, on foot, opened fire, shattering the line of soldiers and killing horses and men. But the relief at seeing the wall of soldiers crumble was blown away as a second charge of soldiers and the Cheyenne scouts slammed into the Nez Percé camp, killing many of them and running off the horse herd that was their only hope of escape. Joseph and many of his men, now on foot, many of them having lost their weapons, tried to recover the herd, racing through a storm of mounted soldiers, a rain of fire coming from above them. Joseph returned on a badly wounded horse, and his oldest wife ran from their tipi, holding what would become the Surrender Gun. Accounts by Helen R. Howard and other historians say that Joseph's wife ran out into the cacophony of the firefight to meet him. "Here's your gun," she yelled, "Fight!" The battle groaned on, charge after charge, sniper fire and explosions—a twelve-pound Hotchkiss gun had been brought to bear, along with a Napoleon gun. That night, an early storm brought five inches of snow and bitter winds. Morning brought no change, a freakish hell of blasting north winds and bleak colors, black smoke, white snow, yellow grass, frozen red blood. It is reported that the gale-force winds let up around noon. The running war was over.

CHAPTER SEVEN
Ned Christie's Model 1873 Winchester Rifle

The fighting had been raging since the first pale light of dawn at Rabbit Trap, Going Snake District, Indian Territory, November 1, 1892. The strange fort on the little bluff above Bitting Creek showed no sign of falling. The lawmen—twenty-five of them, armed with cannon and dynamite and crates of ammunition for their rifles and pistols—had poured over two thousand rifle rounds into the structure. Their cannon had been fired thirty-eight times, the lethal balls of iron and shrapnel and chain screaming into the rock walls, leaving scars, shattering the oak logs, revealing the true strength of the fortifications, which included two thick walls with a layer of sand poured in between. In the lulls the Cherokee warrior and former tribal senator Ned Christie and his

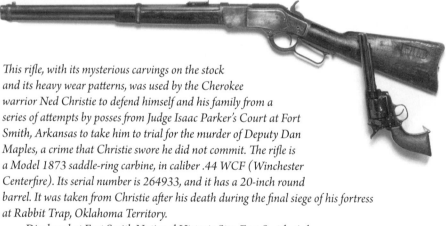

This rifle, with its mysterious carvings on the stock and its heavy wear patterns, was used by the Cherokee warrior Ned Christie to defend himself and his family from a series of attempts by posses from Judge Isaac Parker's Court at Fort Smith, Arkansas to take him to trial for the murder of Deputy Dan Maples, a crime that Christie swore he did not commit. The rifle is a Model 1873 saddle-ring carbine, in caliber .44 WCF (Winchester Centerfire). Its serial number is 264933, and it has a 20-inch round barrel. It was taken from Christie after his death during the final siege of his fortress at Rabbit Trap, Oklahoma Territory.

Displayed at Fort Smith National Historic Site, Fort Smith, Arkansas.

Courtesy Memories by Jody

nephew, Little Arch Wolf, could be heard, gobbling like turkeys, whooping, taunting, calling for the lawmen to bring on the fight. Christie, always on the move, fired his 1873 Winchester from the many gun ports of the fort, showing the same terrifying marksmanship that had made him famous in Indian Territory since he was ten years old.

A deputy, well covered behind an oak tree, braved the rifle fire to recharge the cannon. In frustration he rammed down a double charge of powder. When he touched off the shot, the cannon exploded, the barrel flying apart. A frenzied gobbling came from the fort. The lawmen were growing desperate. Christie's wife, who had escaped the fort during the early hours of the siege, was standing nearby. As a lawman talked with her, boxes of .44 cartridges fell to the ground from hiding places in her dress. Other relatives had gathered, too—Cherokees of the Keetowah Society, the men and women who held on to the old ways in a time of ruthless change and assault. Ned Christie was a hero to many of them, a man of strong family duty, protected by the oldest magic. Watt Christie, Ned's father, refused to help the lawmen negotiate Ned and Little Arch Wolf's surrender, telling them that his son had no evil in him. Even with a posse twenty-five strong, the lawmen could die here, deep in the territory, at the hands of proud people who had been persecuted beyond all human reason. Afternoon faded to twilight, twilight to night, increasing the peril.

Deputies hauled logs and oak planks and bound them to make a bulletproof shield, fixed the shield to the chassis of a wagon, and began rolling it forward in the darkness, preparing dynamite charges as Christie and Little Arch's .44 caliber bullets thudded into the wood, seeking a hole or gap to reach an honored home deep in the living flesh of mortal enemies. The deputies arrived at a place below the fort, safe from the field of fire. One of them lobbed a six-stick dynamite charge at one corner of the structure, and rolled back behind the shield. The explosion lit the night sky, the rock and shattered bits of wood and the sand that had filled the walls visible in the flash, tumbling upward, as if in defiance of all gravity or nature. The debris fell to earth, crashing in the woods where the lawmen and lookers-on crouched. In the silence that followed, the fort began to burn, flames casting wild light and shadows, the sound of the fire building to a roar, a crackling and popping like distant gunfire

Ned Christie leapt from the inferno, his long black hair and clothes afire, and opened fire on the lawmen with his .44 revolvers, one in each hand. The crossfire from so many rifles, aimed by men well hidden in the dark woods, knocked his weapons from his hands, tore at him, and brought him down, his blood watering the same soil where he had been born, thirty-nine years and eleven months before. One of the Cherokee Nation's most ferocious souls flew skyward.

THE STORY OF THE WINCHESTER '73

Ned Christie owned one of the most popular and technologically advanced rifles of his time, known in history as the "Rifle That Won the West," a weapon favored by lawmen and outlaws, Indians and settlers. The Model '73, often saddle-worn, its case-hardened steel components buffed and oiled to satin smoothness, was used in battle by Geronimo's son Chappo, Billy the Kid, and Buffalo Bill Cody, among other notables.

The first Winchester Model 1873s were chambered for Winchester's own .44–40 cartridge, a round specifically designed to address the most serious weakness of the, at the time, still highly sought-after Winchester Model 1866, which fired the relatively anemic .44 Rimfire. The old .44 Rimfire pushed a 210-grain bullet about 1,100 feet per second, about like a modern .357 Magnum revolver. The .44–40 easily adds 700 feet per second to that, pushing a 200-grain bullet to 1,800 feet per second, using a longer cartridge to hold an extra fifteen or more grains of powder. Winchester also offered a revolutionary reloading tool to accompany its new rifle, to make sure that cartridges could be reassembled with efficiency and speed. In most hands the weapon was still useful at only about one hundred to one hundred and fifty yards, but it was a vast improvement. Texas Ranger James B. Gillet bought his Model '73 (paying for the rifle out of his own pocket) in 1875, after almost dying in a running battle with Apaches who already had them. As quoted in *Winchester: An American Legend,* by R. L. Wilson, Gillet wrote that "for the next six years of my ranger career I never used any other weapon. I have killed almost every kind of game that is found in Texas from the biggest old bull buffalo to a fox squirrel with this little Winchester." Buffalo Bill Cody wrote a similar endorsement: "An Indian will give more for one of your guns than any other gun he can get . . . Believe me, that you have the most complete rifle now made."

Oliver Winchester still hoped (as he had with the Model 1866) that the U.S. military would adopt the superior rifle, but the military remained skeptical of repeating rifles in the hands of raw troops, and skeptical of the lever-action design. But the elegant and deadly Model '73s fairly flew out the doors of the factory, in extreme demand from every civilian on the American frontier and across the globe. As with the Model 1866 during the Civil War, any irregular soldier, lawman, or scout (such as the famous Tom Horn in the Apache Wars) who had the money purchased or traded for their own, regulations be damned. The Model '73 could be purchased from the factory for only about $27, with a wide array of accessories available for slightly more cash. A well-heeled rifleman could have his '73 nickel-plated, or even silver- or gold-plated (gold added $10 to the purchase price), or he could have the best walnut stock, checkered by one of the world's experts in the trade, for a few bucks extra. He could buy one of the Trapper's Models, with a barrel only fourteen inches long, which was the highly evolved equivalent of the sawed-off "blanket guns" popular among Indians of the time. Like the "blanket guns," the Trapper's Model was powerful and concealable; unlike them, it was reliable, accurate, repeating, ergonomically efficient in a fight, and held a lot of rounds.

The most accurate '73s (tested on targets at the factory) could be fitted with ultrasensitive set triggers, bringing the first potential for (relatively, remember the limitations of the cartridge) long-range accuracy to a repeating rifle. The range of options that could be factory ordered was very wide—a new and welcome development, since options that proved indispensable in battle or in the field could be incorporated into the standard production rifles as time went on. The top of the line '73s, all options included, were works of art, achieving their zenith with the line of "One in One Thousand" Model 1873s, superfine and customized, usually heavily engraved with scenes of battle or the hunt. These rifles sold for over $100 each, and were held by wealthy owners such as cattle baron Granville Stuart, or presented by the company to notable figures of the time. (The "One in One Thousand" models are among the world's most sought after collector's items now.)

But for most plainsmen, Indians, and gunfighters, such elegant weapons, while probably greatly admired and coveted, were superfluous. They were certainly out of reach for any honest person of average means. By the time the Model 1873s had been transported to the parts of the country where they were most in demand, the price (in Texas, for example, during the wars with the Comanche) was already at $50 for even the most basic model. It could climb from there. Winchester Repeating Arms Company was in a boom. Sales for the company in 1876 totaled almost $2 million, and the company had 690 employees at its bustling factory along the rail yards of New Haven, Connecticut. Military contracts would have made these figures even higher, but in 1876, there was plenty of money to be made in arming the citizenry for the chaos and promise of a frontier suddenly blown wide open.

It would be hard to imagine two more different places than the soot-stained brick factories and clanging rail yards of New Haven, and the lawless hills and dark forested lowlands of Indian Territory, circa 1887, where Ned Christie's story, and his fight to survive, began.

THE STORY OF NED CHRISTIE

The territory began across the Arkansas River from the town of Fort Smith, Arkansas, and extended west through Oklahoma, and north through the southern part of Kansas (the so-called Cherokee Strip that would soon be opened for yet another land rush by white settlers). It was a vast area, western plains and deserts merging to scrub oak forests to majestic hardwoods. It was dotted with isolated and rugged mountain ranges, the Oachitas, the Arbuckles, the Cookson Hills, and traversed by rivers, the Red in the far south, the Canadian, the Neosho, all names that live in American history as the geography of the West's wildest and most lawless era. Through it all ran the mighty Arkansas River itself, a water that crosses between worlds, born a freezing whitewater stream tumbling from the snows of the high Colorado Rockies, drifting across hundreds of miles of dry buffalo country, to empty into the Mississippi at Arkansas's far eastern edge, in a country of cypress swamps, alligators, and Spanish moss.

Ned Christie was born near Tahlequah, Oklahoma, in a settlement called Wauhilla, or Rabbit Trap, on December 14, 1852. His father, Watt Christie, and his mother Thrower Christie, were Cherokee survivors of the "Removal Era" that began in 1825, when the so-called Five Civilized Tribes (Choctaws, Creeks, Cherokees, Chickasaws, and Seminoles) were driven from their homelands by the U.S. government and resettled west of the ninety-fifth parallel. Watt and Thrower had come to the territory on the infamous Trail of Tears in 1838, when seventeen thousand Cherokees from southeastern states were massed in crude concentration camps and then forcibly driven west so that white settlers could claim their lands. At least four thousand Cherokees died in the camps or on the forced march west, among them Ned Christie's grandmother, who was ironically enough, of Irish descent.

Ned Christie came to manhood during a series of armed conflicts within the Cherokee Nation, as two factions of the tribe fought long-running feuds related to the Removal Era. Home burnings and assassinations birthed vengeance killings and constant instability. By the time of the Civil War, which served to divide the Cherokees and other Indian nations even further, the Indian Territory was divided along dozens of fault lines, not just between the tribes but also within them. In such a vacuum of power, the Civil War was even worse than in other parts of the South. Indians who had left their hard-earned settlements and farms to avoid the conflict returned to find the region devastated. Because federal laws did not apply in the territory, the mountain fastnesses and empty prairies also became a magnet and sanctuary for the hordes of lawless wanderers produced by the war, by the mass immigrations from Europe, and by the general ferment of the time. The constant addition of new Indian tribes driven to the territory increased the pressure-cooker atmosphere. Over the years forty different tribes would be resettled there. Peoples as disparate as the Sac and Fox Tribe of the leafy forests of Wisconsin and the warriors of the Everglades, the Seminoles, were forced to live together in the dry, hot, scrub forests and plains. From the West the as-yet unconquered Comanche, Kiowa, and Cheyenne made raids on the often-bewildered newcomers. Many believe that Ned Christie, who was a well-known athlete in everything from stickball to marbles to firearms, learned guerilla warfare in these struggles between the Cherokees and the plains raiders.

The Christies were members of the Keetowah Society, a group of strict Cherokee traditionalists. Ned Christie was a prominent man of the territory, six feet four inches tall, powerfully built, a horseman and a marksman. In his late twenties and early thirties, he was a senator in tribal government, representing his people in the Going Snake District, and an advisor to then-chief Dennis Wolf Bushyhead. During his short life he would be married four times, father and raise children, enjoy the whiskey that flowed like the rivers of the territory, build a blacksmith and gunsmith shop, a sawmill, a farm, and a fort to protect them. He would engage in numerous gun battles, survive ambush and siege, and be accused by U.S. marshals of murder, robbery, liquor smuggling, and horse thievery. But he was never convicted of any crimes. Some historians now say that is because, other than defending his home and family, he never committed any.

It all began May 4, 1887, with the murder of U.S. marshal Dan Maples, shot from his horse on a trail near Tahlequah, while investigating the illegal whiskey trade in the area. Ned Christie was in Tahlequah as part of his duties as a senator—a girl's school had burned to the ground, and the tribal council was determining how and when it should be rebuilt. As was his custom, Christie stayed over to drink and visit with an unruly bunch of friends, among them two whisky traders Bub Trainor and John Parris. The party moved out past a place called Dog Town, into the woods, to a camp near Spring Branch, and it went on all night. Early the next morning, Maples and a deputy came riding by the camp, and somebody from the camp shot him. When Christie recovered from his whiskey late that day, he rode back to town to finish his business with the council. He was shocked to learn that he was a suspect in Maple's shooting, suspicions that increased after John Parris was arrested for the murder, and told anyone who would listen that Christie was the killer. Christie's fellow senators advised him not to trust the law at Fort Smith, and to remain in the territory until they could clear him of suspicion. Christie sent a letter to Judge Isaac Parker in Fort Smith, claiming his innocence, and offering to turn himself in if he could be guaranteed bail, so that he or the marshals could find the real killer. Judge Parker refused the offer.

In 1875 Judge Isaac Parker had come to Fort Smith with orders to clean up the territory, to bring to justice the swarms of killers and bootleggers and fugitives from other regions that were making the territory a misery for more law-abiding Indians, not to mention the thousands of white settlers who had been moving into it. Parker was an almost surreal figure, committed to the law with a religious fervor, a lover of tough debate and the notion that justice could be achieved. He was an orator who delivered his brutal sentences with long and eloquent explanations to the prisoner and the court, drawing on ancient history, the Bible, and classical literature. His advocacy for Indian causes was at the time unusual; it was part of his general conception of what a fair society might be. And part of the idea of fairness was justice for victims. In Judge Isaac Parker's court, that justice often meant hanging. The gallows at Fort Smith was the busiest in the United States, with Parker's grim henchman George Maledon sending seventy-nine men to their deaths, as many as six at a time, over the course of Parker's twenty-one years on the bench.

Isaac Parker ("Hanging Judge" Isaac Parker), in the process of bringing order to the lawless Indian Territories, presided over 13,490 cases in his twenty-one years on the bench, sending seventy-nine souls to his hangman, George Maledon. Ironically, Parker was personally against the death penalty, saying at one point, "I never hanged a man. It is the law."
Courtesy Oklahoma Historical Society

This is the posse that laid siege to Ned Christie's Fort and killed the Cherokee battler, who would later be found to have been innocent of the crime for which he was so relentlessly persecuted and pursued.
Courtesy Oklahoma Historical Society

Parker fully supported an effort to retrieve outlaws from the jurisdiction of tribal courts in the territory to be tried in the "White Man's Court" at Fort Smith. Two hundred U.S. marshals were employed in this effort. Before it ended, sixty-five of them were dead in gunfights. The Cherokee people, whether they were tormented by the outlawry in their land or not, could not help but see the marshals as yet another occupying force. In 1872, during the murder trial of Ezekiel Proctor at the Cherokee court in Tahlequah, a U.S. marshal and a posse of questionable characters actually attacked the courthouse, ostensibly to capture Proctor and drag him back to what they considered the proper courthouse at Fort Smith, which before Parker arrived, was a hotbed of corruption. In the attack on the courthouse, the marshal and his posse were soundly whipped, suffering eight dead and three wounded. From the group that defended the court, three died and six were wounded. Marshals then returned and arrested some of the courthouse defenders and dragged them back to Fort Smith. Proctor escaped.

There was little reason for Ned Christie to believe that he would survive a trial at Fort Smith. He went home to his farm and blacksmith shop. His fourth wife, Nancy Grease, his son James from his previous marriage, and an assortment of kinfolks were living with him. Other kin, and other Keetowah, remained on the lookout for marshals. The Christies got ready for war, and then went back to work around the shop and farm. They did not have to wait long.

The first attempt to serve a murder warrant on Ned Christie took place in late May, right after Judge Parker had refused the request for bail. Deputy Joe Bowers, carrying the warrant, only made it as far as the clearing around the Christie cabin. A bullet from Christie's rifle slammed into his leg. Badly wounded, Bowers fled for his life.

Before the month was out, Deputy John Fields rode in to the Christie farm. According to Bill O'Neal's *Encyclopedia of Western Gunfighters*, Fields was determined to convince Christie to surrender. Christie shot him in the neck with his rifle before he could get close enough to the cabin to speak. Fields survived his wound.

The lawmen waited several months before trying again. This time, they rode in force, a posse large enough to capture any outlaw. But they underestimated their quarry. Christie, fighting alone, struck them like a force of nature. Three lawmen were wounded, and the posse was swiftly routed.

Three years passed. Ned Christie could no longer travel to perform his duties as senator. It has been alleged that he took up outlawry during these years, and that his new crimes were the reason that the famous U.S. marshal Heck Thomas gathered a posse and came for him, yet again, in 1889. Other sources say that Christie spent these years doing what he had been doing for years, raising his children, farming, gunsmithing, wandering the country, when he felt safe, to visit friends and kin.

Heck Thomas's posse took no chances, traveling through the night to reach the Christie farm before dawn. Thomas and two of his men snuck up to the cabin in the dark, only to have the Christie dogs attack them. A rifle shot came immediately from the loft of the cabin, knocking down Marshal L. P. Isbell with a bullet to the arm. In his retreat Heck Thomas set fire to the blacksmith shop by the house. The shop went fast, and the fire spread to the cabin. Nancy and young James Christie made a run for it, as marshals opened up with their rifles. Young James made it to the woods before being shot through the hips and one lung. Christie ran from the cabin, firing with his Winchester at the main posse. Heck Thomas took careful aim and fired and a bullet smashed into Christie's face, breaking through the bridge of his nose and blowing out his right eye. Christie went down, but regained his feet and made it to the cover of the woods.

Over the next year, James and Ned recovered slowly, though Ned would remain disfigured. Relatives and friends gathered to help the family move to the new place on Bitting Creek, where over months they completed what would be referred to in history as Ned's Fort. It was rocked in at the base of the walls, which were made of two layers of oak trees and planks. The space between the layers was filled with sand from the creek bottom. Inside the walls they built a cabin, stocked with provisions and ammunition sufficient to a long siege. Then they built a blacksmith and gunsmith shop. (A photo from this time shows a steam-powered sawmill—top of the line equipment—used to cut and mill the timbers for the fort.)

In 1891 Marshal Dave Rusk rode against the fort with a large force, including a number of Indians. This time, Christie was not alone. From within the fort came a wild gobbling and war cries. Then a storm of rifle fire opened up, flattening four of the posse's men, and sending the rest into retreat.

Rusk, it is reported, could not leave the fort alone. Twice he rode to it, alone, and twice he was repelled by rifle fire. Rusk kept a store in the settlement of Oaks, near Tahlequah. During 1891, it is said, Christie rode into Oaks and burned the store to the ground.

In October of 1892, a posse made up of battle-hardened marshals attacked under cover of darkness. Two of them were shot at the outset of the fight. Those remaining kept up the attack, attempting to set fire to the fort. They hurled dynamite at the walls, but the single sticks of explosives had no effect on the heavy timbers.

Two weeks later, on November 1–2, came the final battle for Ned's Fort. Sam Maples, a man of nineteen at the time, was Marshal Dan Maples's son, and part of the posse that ended Christie's long struggle. As Christie lay dead beside the creek, posse members invited young Maples to avenge his father's murder. Maples walked over and emptied his revolver into the body, firing from only a foot or so away.

Accounts of the end of the battle vary, with some claiming that Ned Christie fought his way out of the burning fort, firing his Winchester only to be killed in the smoke-filled woods by Deputy Wess Bowman. This would account for the Winchester '73 that is shown in the grisly trophy photos of Christie's battered corpse strapped to a door, as his body was freighted by train to Fayetteville, Arkansas, and displayed for crowds and photographers and lawmen. It then made the long trip to Fort Smith for more of the same. Finally, his relatives came and got the body, and carried it back home, to be buried at Rabbit Trap.

In 1918, an eighty-seven-year-old man named Dick Humphrey called the *Daily Oklahoman* to tell the story of a drinking party on Spring Creek, near Dog Town and the murder of Marshal Dan Maples, so long ago. Bub Trainor shot Maples from behind a tree, Humphrey said, near where Christie was sleeping off the drunk of the night before. Trainor then went on to frame Ned Christie by planting evidence—Christie, in the grips of the whiskey, had lost his coat in the woods near where Maples was ambushed, and Trainor had placed the broken-off neck of the whiskey bottle in the pocket of the coat. The neck of the bottle was plugged with a strip of cloth torn from the skirt of the lady bootlegger from whom Christie had bought the whiskey—the evidence was enough to convince marshals that Christie was indeed, the shooter.

Humphrey had waited all these years in terror of Trainor, who went on to become a marshal himself, and then the leader of a criminal gang before being assassinated by four men with shotguns. He died as he had lived, a thoroughly corrupt and murderous man. Ned Christie, even in a half-dozen epic battles with the law, was never known to have killed anybody.

CHAPTER EIGHT
John Wesley Hardin's Colt Double Action
Revolvers Model 1877

On June 3, 2002, these revolvers were sold by the Greg Martin Auction Company to private collectors. The Thunderer was sold for $100,000, the Lightning, $168,000. Released from prison after a sixteen-year term, drinking and gambling hard, trying to write his autobiography and maintain a floundering law practice, Hardin carried his Colt Model 1877 revolvers everywhere he went. He used them to shoot holes in playing cards in El Paso's Washington Park, in a demonstration of his mastery of every kind of handgun skill, from fast draw to twirls and reversals—"border rolls"—exhibiting the deadly accuracy that had taken the lives of forty-four men, almost all of them in personal combat. After shooting the cards in front of a large audience of fellow drinkers, Hardin signed them and swapped them for drinks or gambling chips. The .41 caliber Thunderer shown here was confiscated from Hardin by Deputy Sheriff Will Ten Eyck in the Gem Saloon, on May 6, 1895, after a drunken Hardin used it to rob the Gem Saloon's crap game, where he had sustained a string of heavy losses. It was not the first time he had committed such an act.

The Lightning is short barreled (2½-inch), nickel-plated .38 Caliber, serial number 84304, taken from John Wesley Hardin's body after he was shot to death by Constable John Selman, Sr. in the Acme Saloon, El Paso Texas, at 10 p.m., August 18th, 1895.

The Colt Lightning was given to Hardin as a gift and payment from James "Killin' Jim" Miller, and is inscribed on the grip "JBM to JWH." At the time of the gift, April of 1895, Hardin was practicing law in El Paso, representing Miller in an attempted murder case against Sheriff Bud Frazer, with whom

Courtesy of Greg Martin Auctions

Miller had fought two gun battles, the results of a long-running personal feud. Frazer, a former Texas Ranger, had shot Miller multiple times in both fights, but Miller, who habitually wore a steel plate under his heavy dress coat, survived with minor injuries. Hardin's attempt to prosecute Frazer on Miller's behalf failed. Miller resolved the issue in 1896 by blowing Frazer's head off with a double-barreled shotgun.

Hardin was among the world's most skilled hand-gunners of his time. His letters from prison, and his autobiography, show a man sometimes prone to

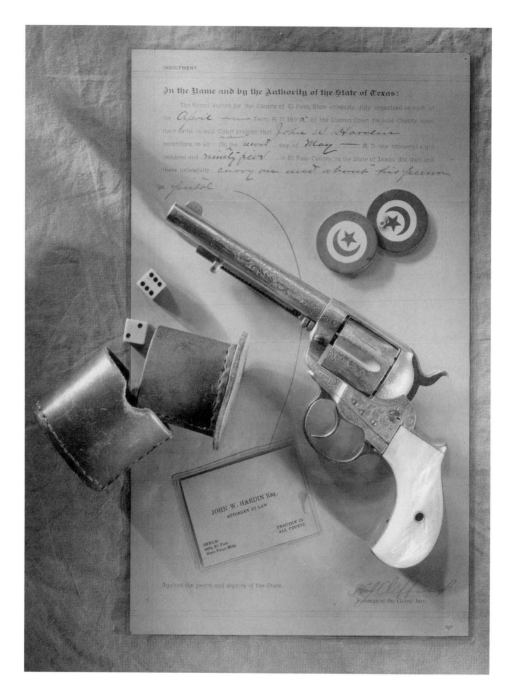

Courtesy of Greg Martin Auctions

megalomania, and one steeped deeply in the Old Testament God of vengeance and blood atonement. There can be little doubt that he reveled in the idea of arming himself with two pistols called the Thunderer, and the Lightning.

El Paso, August 19, 1895

The days were so hot that he just stayed in his room, drinking whiskey and trying to write, to tell how it was back in the spring of 1871, just north of the Little Arkansas River, driving cattle and killing five Mexican vaqueros in one day. Somehow he had to try and get it down, the bullets whirring by his head, thudding and carving the leather on the pommel of his saddle, the cool sweat of it, the way his revolver came to such perfect balance. Stampeding the herd and riding down men, a hilarious cross-fire shot where he and Jim Clements both put a ball through the head of one of the Mexicans, one in each temple, and the way he fell there. It had to be one of the "fightenest" cattle drives in history, and ending up in Kansas, drunk then too, but happy drunk, lean and clear-eyed and not the simplest inch of give in him, luck and fame soaking him like a soft rain in the desert. Faced off over pistols with Wild Bill Hickok in Abilene, then laughing and drinking wine that Hickok paid for. Hickok called him "Little Arkansas," after the fight with the Mexicans. Even Hickok knew better than to try and kill him. He'd shot a feisty drunk for cussing Texans later that day, shot him right in the mouth that had said the words. A week later he hunted down the murdering vaquero Bideno in Sumner County, and killed him with a bullet between the eyes, claiming a purse of $600 for the deed. Kansas had been so good to him, a proud Texas boy of eighteen years, who'd killed twenty-two men. Every few minutes he got up from the old writing desk and drew his Colt Lightning, the gun rising, the front sight covering up the doorknob, or the smeared face of the cowboy in the bad painting on the boardinghouse wall, then the smooth pull to the dry-fire click, again and again, a miracle compared with the old single-actions. He never got tired of it. He poured a fresh drink and sat down, wrote a few words. He'd been pushed all his life, Reconstruction Yankee pillagers and ex-slaves in blue uniforms

*A devout Methodist, nonsmoker, and teetotaler, always impeccably dressed, "Killin'
Jim" or "Deacon Jim" Miller was one of the West's most prolific hired killers, claiming
to have killed nearly fifty men. After hiring Hardin to file charges of attempted murder
against Sheriff Bud Frazer, he paid Hardin with an engraved Colt Lightning and a
pocket watch. Miller is believed to have been the killer of lawman Pat Garrett.*
Courtesy Robert G. McCubbin Collection

killing his kinfolks, trying to run them all like coyotes. Feuds over land or cattle, revenge killings over who killed who when nobody was sober enough to remember who threw the first punch or spat the first insult. He'd put his share of them in the ground, and he wasn't ashamed to write it, or to write most of it, anyway. He had the story roughed out up until 1889, when he was still in prison at Huntsville, studying law and writing to his children, five years still to go on a sixteen-year sentence that might as well have been a lifetime, judging by how it had gone since he'd been free.

When it got too dark to write he left his room, throwing the door open, sudden, Colt Lightning in hand, loaded now. He had enemies everywhere. He went downstairs and began his rounds of the city, past his shadowed law office where his desk lay cluttered with papers and bottles and street dust had drifted a quarter inch thick. He hadn't been in there in weeks. There were bars where he was welcome, and bars where his tab was too long overdue. The bars of Juarez, across the river in Mexico, were too dangerous for him, now. He started out at his favorite place, the Wigwam, but the tab there was getting out of hand. He got into a gambling game at the Gem where he won several pots in a row, big enough to go back and pay off his tab at the Wigwam. He remembered that he'd threatened the life of lawman John Selman Jr. not long before. The boy's father, tough old constable John Selman Sr., had then offered to kill him at some point during the liquor whirl and blur of the days, but it had all dissolved in words. The story is recounted in Leon Metz's *John Wesley Hardin: Dark Angel of Texas.* He'd told Selman Sr. that he didn't have his gun, but when he got it, he'd meet him "smoking, and make you shit like a wolf all around the block." He couldn't remember exactly when that had happened. It was ten o'clock, the desert night cooling, and he went into the Acme, started rolling dice with the bartender and a local grocery store owner named Henry Brown. The dice came up four sixes for him, a lucky roll. "Brown," he said, "you've got four sixes to beat." Nobody knows whether he ever saw old John Selman Sr. step through the open door of the bar and raise his own Colt revolver and open fire. The first bullet was enough. Some say it went in his left eye, some say it came out that way. The bullet traversed his whole brain, exploding it, all the liquor sodden anxieties scrambled, the memories of family and horses and gunfire and endless days of nothing in the stifle and stink of prison. Selman kept on shooting him, through the arm, from chest to back or back to chest, depending on who tells the tale. The coroners who performed the autopsy found another four old bullet wounds on his body, as well as knife scars on his arm and ribs. John Wesley Hardin, the most notorious gunfighter of the West, was dead, at just shy of forty-two years old. He had spent almost sixteen of those years in the penitentiary, and before that, another half dozen on the run. He'd been a free man, a lawyer and writer and a tormented soul, for seventeen and a half months when he was killed. His biographers say that John Selman Sr. did him a favor.

THE STORY OF THE THUNDERER AND THE LIGHTNING

The Thunderer and the Lightning were Colt's first attempts at manufacturing double-action revolvers for mass sale. The double-action revolver dates back to 1851, with the introduction of the Adams, a cap-and-ball pistol in roughly.44 caliber (British 54 bore). The Adams was a beautiful weapon, with several distinct disadvantages—it was expensive, and black powder blowback could burn a shooter's hand, especially after it had been fired many times without cleaning. The long trigger pull to fire it made it inaccurate, and it could not be cocked, it was purely a double-action. But the Adams caught on fast. Its lack of accuracy was not inherent in the weapon; it could be overcome by practice, and the rapid-fire capability of a system that fired the gun and rotated the cylinder to set the next round in front of the firing pin was simply too great an asset. It came of age in a time when Great Britain was involved in violent troubles, where the British colonial empire was being contested by swarms of native-born fighters armed with more primitive weapons, but who had numbers on their side, and the ability to close the distance with troops and take away the advantages of artillery. Rapid fire in a handgun was indispensable.

Using the Adams, British troops and their Gurkha loyalists killed Zulus in the Anglo-Zulu War, in 1879, Russians in the Crimean War of the 1850s, and

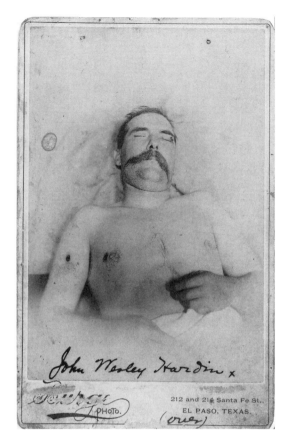

John Wesley Hardin was shot to death by John Selman Sr. on August 19, 1895. Hardin was throwing dice on the bar of the Wigwam Saloon, playing, "Ship, Captain, and Crew," when Selman stepped through the doors. Hardin's last words, before Selman killed him, were "Brown, you've got four sixes to beat...."
Courtesy Robert G. McCubbin Collection

many, many, rebellious sepoys during the Sepoy War (also called the Indian Mutiny) in India in 1857–1858. Small lots of the Adams revolvers found their way to the United States to be used in the Civil War, but it was in the Sepoy Rebellion that the double-action handgun first gained respect as a man-killer.

It was not until 1877 that Colt felt ready to branch out into the new realm of double-action revolvers. The interest had been there, but the 1873 version of the Colt Single Action Army, known as the Peacemaker, in .45 caliber, was arguably the most reliable handgun on earth at the time, a favorite of soldiers from Gen. George Custer to Gen. George Patton, who used his to lethal effect on the Mexican Punitive Expedition of 1916, decades before he would carry a new pair of the revolvers, engraved and custom made, into the killing fields of World War II.

The new Colt Model 1877 Double Actions, the Thunderer, in .41 caliber, and the Lightning, in .38 (an early version, called "The Rainmaker" was made in .32; only a few were produced), ended up being a disappointment to many of their eager purchasers. It was relatively small and very handy, but the double action itself was made up of too many small, fragile parts. The trigger springs often broke under heavy use, or other parts of the mechanism failed under the poor maintenance conditions of the dusty, gritty cattle country. Gunsmiths, it is said, hated the Model 1877s, and they saw a lot of them, turned in for repairs.

The loading system was no improvement over the Peacemaker, either. Cartridges were loaded into the Model 1877s one at a time through a slip aside loading gate (the swing-out cylinder did not appear until the Model 1889) and were ejected using an ejector rod that rested under the barrel. Perhaps the most impressive innovation in the Thunderer was the development of the .41 Long Colt cartridge created specifically for it. It had the ballistics to be a guaranteed man-stopper, but lacked accuracy, and it eventually gave way to the .38, which dominated handgun cartridges at least for the next century.

The 1877s enjoyed an amazing run of production, given their drawbacks. Between 1877 and 1909, when Colt stopped producing them, 166,849 were made. In addition to the Rainmaker, Thunderer, and Lightning, a model in .38, with a 4½-inch barrel, was sometimes sold as "The Storekeeper."

For John Wesley Hardin, his 1877 Thunderer and Lightning were probably treasures, far enough advanced beyond the many handguns and shotguns of his youth before prison as to be technological marvels. Hardin once went into a deadly battle with Mexican cowboys using a cap-and-ball pistol so worn out from his practicing that the only way he could fire it was if he held the cylinder in place with one hand and pulled the trigger with the other. His accounts are filled with misfires, his own, his friends', and his opponents'. In comparison the Model 1877s, whatever their flaws, were near perfect. And Hardin, in El Paso when he owned these weapons, was no cowboy working in clouds of dust, far from gun-cleaning solvent and oil. He was a lawyer and gambler, living in the city, shooting for practice almost every day, and dry firing constantly in his rented room, working and cleaning and oiling his weapons obsessively. The fragility of the guns probably was not an issue for him.

THE STORY OF JOHN WESLEY HARDIN

John Wesley Hardin was born on May 26, 1853, in Bonham, Texas, Fannin County. His father, James Gibson Hardin, was a Methodist preacher, who, like his son John Wesley, would also become a lawyer and a schoolteacher. In a pioneer culture where farming and ranching were the primary occupations, the Hardin family stood out as people of education, if not wealth. John Wesley had nine brothers and sisters. Hardin's mother was widely respected, the daughter of a doctor who had come to Texas from Indiana.

Young Hardin grew up around Central Texas, and was a self-described "child of nature," hunting and fishing, happiest out in the swamps and thickets, and almost always in the company of the black families who worked for his uncles on their small ranches. He has been described as an outspoken racist, but it is likely that he was far less racist than was the norm in his time and place. During the lead-up to the Civil War, his father had voted against Texas secession, an unpopular, if very rational, vote. But when the war came, the Hardin family threw its unequivocal support behind the South. At the age of nine, John Wesley made an attempt at "running off" to kill Yankees, afire with the furious rhetoric of the day: Abraham Lincoln was burned in effigy in the squares of the dusty little makeshift towns, and personal honor was both paramount, and equated with the honor of the South itself. "The way you bend a twig, it will grow," wrote Hardin in his autobiography, "is an old saying, and a true one. So I grew up a rebel."

And it was more than just the fires of war that guided John Wesley Hardin. He witnessed his first murder when he was eight, a poor old man hounded and humiliated by a younger, wealthier one, for a debt that he could not pay—the poor man's honor saved when he beat his way through a crowd and slashed

John Wesley Hardin at eighteen years old, in his fighting and killing prime, in Abilene, Kansas, 1871. At the time of this photo, according to biographer Leon Metz, Hardin had already killed twenty-two men in gunfights.

Printroom.com Photography

his tormentor's throat with his bowie knife. Hardin would soon be in a knife fight of his own, in the schoolyard, at age thirteen, with a boy named Charles Sloter who, unforgivably, chalked some offensive graffiti on a wall himself and then accused Hardin of it. "I proved it up on him" Hardin wrote, by stabbing Sloter, almost fatally, in the chest and back. It was deemed by the teachers and authorities a case of righteous vengeance, and dismissed.

Righteous vengeance was the order of the time. And when the Civil War ended, the true humiliation of the South—and the thirst for vengeance in some parties on both sides—began. Reconstruction–era laws were bitterly resented in Texas, as were the troops—many of them ex-slaves from other states—brought in to enforce them. Texans who had lived far from the major fighting of the war, who were settlers accustomed to making their own rules, who had fought Comanches, renegades, and Mexican soldiers and raiders with no help from outside, suddenly were faced with an extremely hostile occupying force.

In 1868 Hardin and a cousin—both of them fifteen—got into a wrestling match with an ex-slave named Mage, the former property of Hardin's uncle, now a free and proud man who had yet to ponder the limits of freedom. The wrestling match started in good fun, two boys trying to pin a powerfully built man who prided himself on his skill. But it ended in fury, with Mage threatening to kill Hardin, for scratching his face. Insult was added when Hardin's uncle broke up the fight and ordered Mage off his farm.

The next morning, Mage stopped Hardin in the road and grabbed his horse's bridle, and Hardin, as he describes in his autobiography, "shot him loose" with a Colt .44, causing wounds that would soon kill him. It was an avoidable tragedy, like so many of those that came on its heels.

The Hardin family knew that the penalty for killing an ex-slave would be hanging, and that under Reconstruction law, there would be no fair trial. They encouraged John Wesley to run. He wrote in his autobiography, "I became a fugitive, not from justice, be it known, but from the injustice and misrule of the people who had subjugated the South." He did not run far, or try to hide very well, and when troops came for him, he ambushed them at a ford on a creek, opening the fight with a shotgun, and finishing it with a cap-and-ball revolver. He was slightly wounded in the arm but killed four men.

In a violent time, a well-armed, gun-obsessed young man of seventeen, bursting with pride, hunted by an occupying enemy, with a record of kills, would be a romantic figure, and Hardin was aware of the figure he cut. Gambling, probably stealing the occasional horse, taking work for relatives when he was broke, he built a reputation as a man who would not back down. He murdered a young man over a gambling conflict, and may even have hunted down and killed the judge who indicted him for that slaying. Challenged by a muscled-up performer at a nighttime campfire party, Hardin shot the man in the face with his .45. Captured by three lawmen near Longview, Texas, Hardin bided his time, played the part of a terrified seventeen-year-old boy, and, when they let down their guard, killed them all.

No longer at ease as a fugitive in Texas, Hardin signed on with his cousins the Clements, to drive a herd of cattle north, eighty days of travel, to the railheads of Abilene, Kansas, up the Chisholm Trail, through Indian Territory, and across a no-man's land that will forever be synonymous with the Wild West. It was a blood-soaked drive, far more so than most others of the time. Hardin began it by shooting a white ox that would not leave the herd of cattle, and for which he had to pay $200 to the owner, who lived near the trail. He killed an Osage Indian who tried to take a "tax" of a steer from the herd. At the Little Arkansas River, a team of Mexican cowboys tried to drive their herd past Hardin and the Clements' cattle, and a serious gunfight broke out. Six of the Mexicans were killed, five of them by Hardin. By the time the herd reached Abilene, describes historian and writer Leon Metz, stories of John Wesley Hardin, the boy who "thinned out" Union troops in Texas and "killed men just to see them kick," were being told in all of the bars and brothels, which were some of the rowdiest, most dangerous watering holes in the world at the time.

The marshal of Abilene at that time was Wild Bill Hickok. Bets were placed that the Texas boy that people were calling "Little Arkansas" after the fight there, would face down or kill Hickok. At thirty-four years old, Hickok was a

John Selman Sr., was devoted to his sons. John Jr., the child pictured here, grew up to join his father as a lawman in rowdy El Paso. When a drunken John Wesley Hardin threatened John Selman Jr., Selman Sr. killed Hardin, and was acquitted of murder. Selman was later killed in a shootout with fellow lawman, George Scarborough. Hardin biographer Leon Metz notes that the X inscribed on Selman's crotch in this photo was put there by El Paso prostitutes who had access to the photo.
Courtesy James H. Earl

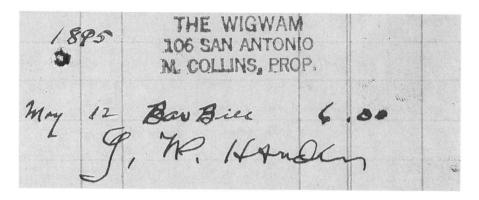

One of Hardin's bar tabs
Courtesy Robert G. McCubbin Collection

man in his prime, and one who inspired both respect and fear in Abilene. He was not without enemies, but most of them were afraid of him. Texan Phil Coe hated him because he had been a Union scout, and because, when Coe and his fellow gunman Ben Thompson opened Abilene's notorious Bull's Head Saloon, they paid an artist to paint a huge bull on the wall outside, complete with giant testicles and penis. More orderly citizens complained, and Hickok, rather than forcing the issue, simply painted over the offensive genitalia himself.

Hardin would always say that when Hickok came to him on the streets of Abilene and tried to arrest him for wearing his guns in town, he had handed his pistols, butt first to the famous marshal, then performed the "border roll," reversing the guns and cocking them, ready to kill Hickok. Accounts differ on what happened but are certain on the outcome. Hickok befriended Hardin, who was allowed to carry his guns openly in Abilene, a privilege denied all other cowboys. And he took advantage of it. On the same day he met Hickok, he shot a man who came into a restaurant, cursing Texans, shot him in the mouth. A week later, he hunted down and killed a Mexican, who was wanted for murder, and received a purse of $600 from local citizens for the deed. It may have been with this money that he bought the suit he is wearing in the famous photo of him in Abilene. His welcome in the violent cow town was revoked when he killed Charlie Cougar at the American House Hotel, allegedly to stop him from snoring.

Back in Texas in 1872, Hardin became embroiled in the Sutton-Taylor Feud, on the side of the Taylors. He married Jane Bowen, was wounded in a gun battle over gambling and insults, killed a man named Jim Cox and then another, Jack Helm, who had been recruited by federal authorities to bring members of the Taylor faction to justice, and who had been implicated in the summary execution of prisoners. Not to mention Sheriff Charlie Webb of Comanche, among others.

But the tide had turned. Reconstruction was over, and Texas was again, while still very unruly, self-governed. The citizens were exhausted by conflicts like the Sutton-Taylor Feud, and by the many young desperadoes, exemplified by John Wesley Hardin, who caused a terrible sense of dread in whatever towns they visited. The citizens of Comanche petitioned the new governor for Texas Rangers to come and capture Hardin and his fellow gunmen. Hardin's father and brother Joe were arrested, along with some of their friends. John Wesley and Jim Taylor, surprised at their camp, fought it out and escaped. In the wake of several such battles, Joe Hardin and two friends were taken from the jail in Comanche and lynched. Hardin, after riding the country with a heavily armed band of loyalists, hoping for revenge, eventually decided to take his wife and run, hoping to preserve his father's life by leaving Texas.

He was captured on a train in Pensacola, Florida, on August 23, 1877, in a wild brawl. His attempt to draw his Colt .45 was foiled when the revolver snagged in his suspenders. Texas Ranger John Barclay Armstrong beat Hardin senseless with the butt of his own revolver.

The costs of Hardin's youthful violence—and it has never been suggested that he was a thief or robber or other type of criminal, merely a young man who never refused a challenge, and who happened to win almost all of them—were to be paid the rest of his life. He continued to write Jane and his three children all the many years he was in prison, but she seldom wrote him back, or even visited him very often. It is clear that he suffered greatly: He was flogged after escape attempts, placed in solitary, his old gunshot wounds tortured him with abscesses and bone pain, and he almost died of an illness in 1884 and 1885. In letters included in Metz's *Dark Angel of Texas,* Hardin wrote to Jane of "disgraceful" episodes in which he took part, "something I cannot mention." He worked in prison as a cobbler and quilt maker, studied law, taught Sunday school.

Jane died in 1892, at age thirty-five, two years before Hardin gained his release from Huntsville Penitentiary. His children were cared for by a family friend, rancher Fred Duderstadt. Hardin left prison and passed the Texas bar exam in 1894, and moved to El Paso, a town where many of the lawless were finding their last sanctuary. He married a fifteen-year-old girl, Callie Lewis, who was infatuated with his reputation. However, the marriage lasted only a week, and Callie went home to her parents. Although he practiced law in El Paso (among his clients were members of the local Mexican community, outlaws, and his relative by marriage, James "Killin' Jim" Miller), he drank and gambled like a man possessed, taking up with an ex-prostitute named Beulah M'Rose, the wife of a local badman, Martin M'Rose, who would soon be found murdered on the bridge between El Paso and Juarez.

Beulah and Hardin occupied a rooming house in downtown El Paso, where they worked together on Hardin's autobiography. Beulah seems to have been a good writer, and a person of education; the book's polished qualities have been attributed to her work. But she was as wild and prone to hell-raising as her new man-friend. The couple drank whiskey by the gallon, and fought like wildcats. One morning, Beulah went wandering the streets of the city, drunk and disorderly, and ran afoul of lawman John Selman Jr., who arrested her and took away her two Colt .41 revolvers. Hardin bailed her out, furious at Selman, threatening him with death.

After days of drunken fighting, Beulah finally left Hardin, then came back, then left for good, heading for California with her young son. Hardin descended further after her departure. He got into a street argument with John Selman Sr. who'd confronted him about his threats to Selman's son.

Selman Sr. was a constable for the city, a grizzled fifty-seven-year-old man with a long past, and a reputation of his own. He had been an early rancher in West Texas, fought Apaches and Comanches, and had been the leader of an outlaw gang called the Selman's Scouts, robbing and stealing cattle on both sides of the border. He and his "scouts" had done battle with Texas Rangers and U.S. troops. In 1895, when he began to have trouble with John Wesley Hardin, he had been constable of El Paso for three years. He was devoted to his son, and probably afraid that Hardin might kill him if it came to a fight.

On August 19, Hardin made the rounds of the bars, from the Wigwam to the Gem and on to the Acme. As he was throwing dice along the bar, Selman Sr. stepped through the open doors and shot him down with a Colt .45, probably a Single Action Army.

Among Hardin's effects recorded by the coroners were his Colt Lightning handgun (reports say two Colts were on the body, others say only one), and a new garnet ring, inscribed by his children and given to him as a gift for his forty-first birthday.

Selman was tried for the killing, but the trial resulted in a hung jury. Before the second trial could be scheduled, a drunken Selman Sr. got into a fight with fellow lawman George Scarborough—it has long been believed that Hardin had paid several men to kill Martin M'Rose, among them Scarborough and Selman, and there was bad blood about the way the pay had been split up— and Scarborough shot him seven times, killing him. (Scarborough was in turn killed by Wild Bunch member Harvey Logan four years later.)

CHAPTER NINE
Tom Horn's Winchester Model 1894 Rifle

At the time that Horn owned his .30–30 Winchester, it was a top-of-the-line piece of lethal equipment, in the hands of one of the West's most lethal men. It was shipped from the Winchester factory on June 19, 1900, and may have been purchased by Horn with the profits from his killing of rustlers—he charged cattlemen an alleged $600 per man. More than likely, however, the rifle was purchased by members of the Wyoming Stock Growers Association, and given to their hired guns, of whom Tom Horn remains the most famous, and the most controversial. While the exterior of the rifle looks to be in excellent condition, the bore exhibits an extreme amount of wear, perhaps due to use after Charles Irwin took possession of it, or perhaps because Tom Horn, like Wild Bill Hickok and other gunfighters, was obsessive about his own shooting practice.

This Winchester Model 1894 .30 caliber (known as the .30–30 Winchester), serial number 82667, was owned by Tom Horn, Army scout, man-hunter for the Pinkerton Agency, "cattle detective" in Wyoming and Colorado. Horn gave this rifle to his friend, Wyoming rancher Charles (C. B.) Irwin, three days before Horn was hanged at Cheyenne, Wyoming, on November 20, 1903. The rifle was displayed at the National Cowboy Hall of Fame in Oklahoma City, Oklahoma, and is now believed to be back in the hands of the Irwin family.
Courtesy National Cowboy & Western Heritage Museum

Horn was suspected in the sniper-style murders of rustlers and settlers suspected of cattle stealing throughout the Chugwater River country of Wyoming from 1895 through 1899, when he apparently moved south to the Brown's Hole region of extreme northern Colorado, an area he knew well from hunting outlaws during his Pinkerton Agency days. Mysterious, sniper-style killings of several cattle rustlers in that area (including Matt Rash and Isam Dart), were attributed to Horn, though never proven. Sometime in early 1901, ill with malaria from his recent volunteer service in the Rough Riders during the Spanish-American War, Horn returned to the Chugwater and recovered at the ranch of his old friend, cattle baron John C. Coble. Horn also picked up his chosen profession of cleaning out rustlers and suspicious nesters by killing and terrorizing them with the constant threat of a bullet from nowhere. Those bullets were almost certainly delivered from his Winchester Model 1894. Whether this rifle was the one used to murder young Willie Nickell, the crime for which Tom Horn was hanged, is a matter that has been debated now for well over a hundred years.

THE STORY OF THE WINCHESTER MODEL 1894 WINCHESTER

The Winchester Model 1894 was the culmination of lever-gun technology, perhaps the last word on the subject. For a long time after the introduction of the Model 1894 to the West, any lever gun was referred to as a "Winchester" (just as later refrigerators would all be called "Frigidaires," regardless of the manufacturer). The Model 1894 introduced a series of firsts to the already venerable lever-gun tradition. Most important, it was the first lever gun designed to use cartridges burning "smokeless" powder, a product that had evolved from early experiments with "guncotton," an explosive created from wood or cotton fibers soaked in nitric and sulfuric acid. Guncotton had been discovered in the 1840s, and had found use as an explosive and propellant in cannons, but it was also unstable. After several factories producing it in Europe exploded with great loss of life, guncotton had been relegated to the pile of promising but impractical inventions. French chemists, and explosives visionaries such as Alfred Nobel in Great Britain, continued to explore the possibility that guncotton could be stabilized enough to be used on the battlefield. By the 1880s such explorations were paying off. French chemists introduced a substance called "Poudre B," a stabilized version of guncotton, and with it, in 1886, French gunsmiths produced the first military weapon to utilize the new propellant. The Lebel Model 1886 was a bolt-action rifle firing an 8 millimeter bullet (originally 231 grains, later lightened to 197) at mind-blowing velocities of over 2,300 feet per second, and capable of delivering a lethal blow to an enemy at 4,500 meters. The new smokeless powder produced three times the power of the old black powder, left no burnt residue to foul barrels and bog down moving parts. It left no telltale cloud of smoke to identify a sniper's nest, or to completely fog a battlefield during massed engagements, which had been one of the major problems of the warfare of previous decades. The invention of smokeless powder was a revolution in firearms technology that allowed the other revolutions—especially in fully automatic weapons, with their complex mechanisms susceptible to fouling and jamming—to unfold.

The .30 Winchester Center Fire (WCF) cartridge that came to dominate American deer hunting (and not a little bit of man hunting) was not Winchester's first choice for the Model 1894. The rifle was first chambered for the .32–40 and .38–55 black powder cartridges, but these gave way to the .25–35 and the .30–30 (30-caliber bullet pushed by 30 grains of powder) loaded with the new smokeless. In the .30–30, the rifle delivered excellent if not shocking ballistics. The first cartridges were loaded with 160-grain bullets that flew at just shy of 2,000 feet per second. The bullet dropped fast—almost two feet in 300 yards—but it was still moving at almost 1,400 feet per second, and carrying around 800 foot pounds of energy, more than enough to kill a man (it is equivalent to being shot point-blank with a Korean War–era M-1 Carbine). By comparison to other weapons of the time, the 1892 issue .30–40 Krag— the world's first military-issued, magazine-fed bolt-action rifle—carried a bit hotter round (with 40 grains of smokeless pushing the .30 caliber bullet), and a heavier (220 grains) bullet. It was chosen for the American campaign against the Spanish in Cuba and the Philippines, once again proving that the military simply was not going to trust the lever guns. But there is little doubt that many of the Rough Riders who volunteered with Theodore Roosevelt to go to Cuba to fight in 1898—so many of them westerners, including Tom Horn—would have preferred the Winchester Model 1894 in .30–30, for its superb handling characteristics, reliability, and most of all, familiarity. Since the introduction of the Henry, and then the Winchester Model 1866, westerners had lived, hunted, fought, and died with a Winchester lever gun in their hands.

For some years the Winchester Company, recognizing that most of their customers could afford only one rifle, and that those customers were overwhelmingly buying the Model 1894 in .30–30, produced a small game load for the rifle, so that a hunter out looking for deer could take rabbits or birds without grave loss of meat or expense. The load came with a one-hundred-grain bullet pushed with only six grains of smokeless powder.

The Model 1894 has been in production for over one hundred years, with almost six hundred thousand rifles, most of them in .30–30 caliber, sold across the world. It holds the honor of being the most successful civilian rifle in history, in constant production for over a century.

CHUGWATER RIVER COUNTRY, NEAR IRON MOUNTAIN, WYOMING, SUMMER OF 1895

Nobody could say that there was no warning. The notes had been tacked to the doors of makeshift shacks and dugouts all through the valley of the Chugwater. Stop stealing cattle, leave, or die. Many of the settlers tried to leave the cattle barons' herds alone, even though it was becoming obvious to them that the land was too high and cold and raw for farming. The wild game was mostly shot-out, and hopes for long-term survival were few. The railroads selling "rain follows the plow" flimflams and the Wyoming land agents showing photos of bumper crops taken in places that were not Wyoming had all lied, and the settlers were stuck. Short-term survival would have to suffice. Sometimes that meant taking down a cow or two in a lonely coulee, or bunching a few and using a "running iron" to change the brands for a quick sale.

William Lewis was one of the settlers that got two notes. He laughed at them both. Lewis never made a pretense of farming as other rustlers in the area had done. He plowed no ground, bought no seed. He lived in a tiny crude cabin and built crude corrals, filled them with cattle and horses roped on the vast open ranges weakly controlled by the local cattle barons. (Cattle rustling was so common at the time that it had its own vocabulary: stealing cows was called "throwing the long rope" and unbranded calves, ripe for the taking, were called "slicks.") No one seemed to know where Lewis had come from, but he was a man of temper and violence, a man who was always armed and who was described as living without friendship. He had been arrested once for stealing cattle, and had been freed by a jury of men much like himself, hard men, hard up, trying to survive. No matter how much power the Wyoming Stockgrowers Association might hold over the country, a new power had poured in, poor men, settlers, who were not about to hang one of their own, whether they liked him or not.

The deadline for leaving stated in the warning notes had come and gone, a subject of mockery by some of the hard men of the Chugwater.

In the early morning, out by the corrals, the first bullet struck with a thud beside Lewis's boot, scuffing a divot from the hard-packed earth and raising the tiniest puff of dust. The rifle shot that followed was a clear, short bang, lost so quickly in the immensity of sand rock and dry grassland that Lewis could not tell where it came from.

He mounted his horse and drew his pistol, riding the perimeter of his land, looking for the bushwhacker, or a clue to where he had lain in ambush. There was nothing, not a track, not a spent cartridge. A few days later, a hot and still August midmorning, as he worked to put rails on his corral, another bullet thunked into a fencepost. This time, Lewis had his rifle at hand, and he fired at the empty landscape, selecting spots where a rifleman might be concealed. After some hours searching the country for his assailant, he made a circuit of the neighbors, brandishing the rifle, telling them that he was ready for attack, eager for the fight and the kill of the cowardly assassin that had tried to kill him and couldn't get the job done. Perhaps Lewis thought that the coming fight would be a chance for vengeance, a chance to strike a blow for the little man, honest or otherwise. It was not impossible; the Wyoming Stockgrowers Association and a band of almost fifty hired killers had taken on the settlers and come out on the losing end of the Johnson County War, in April of 1892, in the Powder River country.

But the time for that kind of conflict was over. The ranchers had learned valuable lessons in the public debacle of the Johnson County War. A new order had come into the barren valley of the Chugwater, one that rode alone by night, lay in silent ambush by day, left no tracks, no sign of its constant watching.

The warning time was over, too. When William Lewis went out to his corrals early the next morning, a bullet struck him in the center of his sternum and blasted away his heart. He clung to the rails, and a second shot struck him in the side, knocking him to his knees. A third rolled him out flat. Nobody found him for three days. When news of the killing got out, Lewis's neighbors told reporters that it was a relief to have him dead.

The next killing came two weeks later.

Fred Powell's final note read like this: "Laramie, Wyo., September 2, 1895 Mr. Powell—this is your third and last warning. There are three things for you to do—quit killing other people's cattle or be killed yourself, or leave the country yourself at once."

Even according to his hired hand, Andy Ross, would-be rancher Fred Powell was "mighty crude in the way he took in cattle." Powell had lost an arm while working on the railroad, but that had not stopped his career as an unrepentant thief and general malefactor. He brazenly stole horses and cattle, even from neighbors who were as poor as he was. Ross and Powell were cutting willows in a creek bottom about twelve miles from the Lewis cabin, getting ready to build hay racks for the season's last crop of hay. It was September 10, 1895.

The shot came from far away, Ross said. Powell took the bullet in the chest, and died in the creek bottom.

The killings had an effect on the Chugwater. Settlers who had come to rely on free cattle to help them get by until they could establish farms or ranches of their own left. So did others who were sure that they would be targeted whether they stole cattle or not, just as innocents had been lynched in the Johnson County War. True rustlers left, too, unable to concentrate on catching cattle and using a "running iron" to change their brands. All that work, out in the open, a fire burning to heat the irons, the cattle bawling, dust rising, could not be done with a professional assassin lurking, apparently able to turn up anywhere at any time. It is said that a rider in the Chugwater during these years could witness the fruits of Tom Horn's labors: dugouts stood empty with doors agape, weed-grown cabins abandoned and yawing in the wind, over all hung a desolate silence.

The new order seemed to be working out just as the cattlemen had hoped it would.

THE STORY OF TOM HORN

Tom Horn was born at the very outset of the Civil War, and came of age in the bitter years of the 1870s, on a small farm in Scotland County, Missouri. In his autobiography, written from his jail cell, he describes leaving home after his faithful dog, Shedrick, was shot dead after having attacked a boy who was beating Horn—and after one too many severe beatings from his father. He drifted west, worked as a stage driver and mail rider, and, at age sixteen, entered the world of the Apache Wars in Arizona. He was a natural linguist and he learned Spanish and Apache over a matter of months, drawing wages as an interpreter for the army and others. It is said that he spoke German, also, which he may have learned from his mentor among the Apaches, Al Sieber, the German-born "Chief of Scouts" for the army. Sieber was renowned for his honesty, his intelligence, and his brutality.

The Apache Wars would be the refining fire of Horn's life, taking him into battle from sun-blasted deserts deep in Mexico to the high mountains of Arizona, through a maze of politics and betrayals by Indian agents, soldiers, Apaches, Mexicans, and crooked civilians on both sides of the border. Those years also took him deep into Apache warrior culture, an experience that

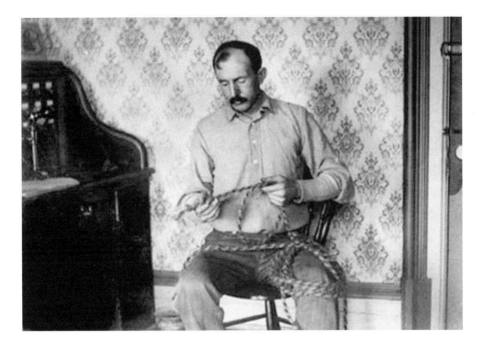

A rodeo star and cowboy as well as a man hunter, Tom Horn spent his days in prison braiding horsehair lariats, talking with friends, and planning his escape.
Courtesy of James D. Julia Auctions, Fairfield, Maine

probably marked him for life. He is said to have been an interpreter at the surrender of Geronimo, and a witness to the tragic mistreatment of the Apaches afterward.

At twenty-seven years old, he had ridden in one of the West's most challenging campaigns, in some of the world's most difficult terrain, against some of the world's fiercest warriors. It was difficult to know what to do next. He had served with men like Al Sieber and the Medal of Honor winner (and medical doctor) Maj. Gen. Leonard Wood, who was called "Old Icebox" for his demeanor in battle. Horn tried mining (in some of the most dangerous Apache country left), but wrote later in his autobiography that, "it was too slow, and I could not stay at it." He won purses at rodeos and at roping contests, and in April of 1887, he wandered into the Pleasant Valley War, a war

of annihilation between the Graham family of cattlemen and the sheepherd-
ing Tewksbury family. Horn served as deputy under Yavapai County Sheriff
Bucky O'Neil during the feud, and it is believed that he worked as a hired
gunman in the war. Horn wrote in his autobiography that he served as "media-
tor" in the conflict, which he described, in what is probably a clue as to whom
he served, as a "war to the knife between cattlemen and rustlers." He also
served as deputy under Apache County Sheriff Commodore Owens, who
while attempting to make an arrest for a murder related to the feud, killed four
members of the Graham faction in a blistering gunfight that lasted only a few
minutes. The Pleasant Valley War ended in 1892 after both families had basically killed each other off.

By then Tom Horn was working for the Pinkerton Agency, as a professional manhunter and tracker. He was dogged and certain in his pursuits,
often working undercover, posing as a rustler or drifting cowhand, and riding
from Colorado to Indian Territory in Oklahoma and back again, bringing in
train robbers and cattle rustlers. In the early spring of 1894, the Pinkertons
sent Horn to Wyoming to investigate organized cattle and horse stealing in
Colorado and Wyoming, where he first met John Coble and other prominent
stockmen of the region. Coble and other ranchers were facing a sea change in
the livestock industry. Homesteaders—the stockmen hated them and called
them "nesters"—were staking claim to the most productive rangelands and
creek bottomlands in southern Wyoming and northwest Colorado. They

Another of Horn's weapons. Look closely at the inscription.
Photo courtesy James D. Julia Auctions, Fairfield, Maine

blocked cattles' access to water, and built their farms where the ranchers cut their hay. Many of them were stocking their claims with sheep, which cattlemen were convinced would ruin the land by grazing the earth bare. Furthermore, the homesteaders saw little harm in taking in "stray cattle." When that tolerant attitude toward thievery led to an influx of professional rustlers to the area, some homesteaders saw that as a positive development, hurting the big ranchers who despised them.

The tolerance for the criminals proved to be an Achilles heel for the settlers, as did the settlers' habit of serving on juries and turning loose men accused of rustling. The cattlemen, accustomed to being the power, found instead that the legal system was closed to them. Hiring the respected manhunter and their friend, Tom Horn, to post warnings on the doors of cabins in the area, and to murder those who would not be warned, was their solution. The pay was good—as high as $600 per kill—and the life was much more free than his employment with the Pinkertons, which Horn had often said that he did not like. (Some reports say that the Pinkerton Agency quietly fired him after he was suspected of a robbery in Nevada.) It is estimated that Horn killed between twenty-five and thirty men during his career as a "stock detective," all of them shot sniper style, or, in the parlance of the day, "dry-gulched." The cattlemen needed an "angel of death," as Horn would come to be called in the accounts of the day, and nobody could have been better for the job.

Restless as always, in 1898, Horn joined up with the Rough Riders to fight and serve as pack master (handling mules) in the Spanish-American War, under the command of Theodore Roosevelt, Maj. Gen. Leonard "Old Icebox" Wood, and Yavapai County Sheriff Bucky O'Neill. It must have felt like a reunion. Hundreds of western plainsmen were heading to Florida to fill the ranks of the wild and illustrious dream army of war-mad Teddy Roosevelt. The outcome of the Rough Riders adventure was a glorious victory in Cuba, but the costs of the expedition were high, over three thousand U.S. soldiers dead of fever or other disease, and another two hundred killed or wounded. Eighty-nine of the Rough Riders fell. Horn, it is believed, never saw combat, falling ill with malaria in Cuba. Bucky O'Neill, exhorting his soldiers at the

Battle of Kettle Hill, took a Spanish Mauser round (propelled by the new smokeless powder) in the mouth that blew his brains out the back of his head. His last comment, before he was hit, was that there was no Spanish bullet made that could kill him.

Horn returned to Wyoming from Florida, still weak from fever, and recovered at his friend Coble's ranch. Whatever his relationship with the Pinkerton Agency, Horn became fascinated with the Union Pacific train robbery that took place on June 2, 1899, and while in pursuit of the robbers (probably in pursuit of the reward for their capture), he took the opportunity to earn some extra cash by killing rustlers in the Brown's Hole area of northern Colorado (now Brown's Park National Wildlife Refuge just south of Highway 319).

The train robbers, members of the Wild Bunch, eluded him (although one of the rustlers Horn shot on this trip was loosely connected to the gang). But his work as a hired killer was lucrative. It was during this time that he was alleged to have begun his custom of marking his kills by putting a small rock under the heads of the dead men. The legend may not be true, but it has the ring of truth to it, because Horn's campaign was to introduce terror to the region, and symbols—first the notes and then the rocks—held the power to terrify. Horn would later brag that he had stopped cow stealing in his region in one single year of "work."

It was the bragging that would bring him down. In the ultraposh saloons of Cheyenne and Denver, where Horn went on multiday sprees, drinking and patronizing the brothels with the money he made, he liked to talk. He bragged to adoring audiences of three-hundred-yard kills, of multiple shots made very fast, of the terror he brought to the nesters and their ilk on behalf of his friends, powerful and important men of industry, all of them. Out of money, and sober again, he rode away from these modern, gas-lit cities and into the plains, and went back on the hunt, silent, living on almost nothing, sleeping cold, waiting for the kill, just as he had been doing almost his entire life.

In 1900, while working for John Coble, Horn found what was probably the first girlfriend of his life. In his wanderings over the ranges, he often spent the night with the Miller family, a rough-and-tumble outfit building a ranch near Iron Mountain. The Millers were friends with Coble, and they provided the board for the schoolteacher of the Iron Mountain School, a Missouri-born woman named Glendolene Kimmell, who had come to the West, she would say later, out of an affinity for adventure and the frontier type. She complained that most of the men she encountered in Wyoming were little different than the field and factory hands she had known in the East. When Tom Horn drifted in to the Miller Ranch, she recognized an altogether different breed.

Horn was forty-one, Kimmell, twenty-two. From her later writings it was clear that her sympathies lay with the powerful cattlemen and with the wild and romantic figure of Tom Horn rather than with the nesters and homesteaders who were crowding the land. She was also fearless in her own way—many people warned her away from her job at the Iron Mountain School because it was at the center of a decade-long blood feud between the Millers and the Nickell family, a clan of Kentuckian homesteaders who had settled on North Chugwater Creek. The patriarch of the family, Kels Nickell, was a veteran of the Plains Indian Wars, a man who had watched his own father murdered by guerillas in the last days of the Civil War. Kels was a hard-bitten man who refused to be pushed at all. Almost as if to spite his neighbors, Nickell ran sheep on his homestead and on the land he was purchasing. His temper was locally feared, and rightly so: In an 1890 dispute over grazing on John Coble's land, Kels Nickell pulled a knife and badly wounded Coble. Both families in the feud, like most people in the Chugwater at this time, went armed at all times.

It was clear that someone was going to be killed. Descendants of the Nickells say that on July 10, 1901, a threatening note was left on the Nickells' gate. Kels Nickell did not scoff at the note. But he did not consider leaving the ranch he had built up to relative prosperity over sixteen years of backbreaking toil, either. Everybody in the country knew what had happened to Rash and Dart, but those men were professional criminals. Kels did not believe that anybody would try to kill a father of eight young children who owned his own section of land, just because he was a sheepman with few friends. He was wrong.

Eight days later, Willie Nickell rode out early, on his father's horse, to meet a new hired hand at the railroad stop. The morning was chilly, and he

A schoolteacher from Missouri almost twenty years younger than Tom Horn,
Glendolene Kimmell came to Wyoming in search of adventure and tough, independent
"frontier-types." She was disappointed until she met Tom Horn, who had lived a life
beyond her imagination.

Courtesy University of Wyoming, American Heritage Center

wore his father's coat and hat. The boy dismounted to open a gap gate and lead his horse through. Two bullets from a .30–30 hit him in the back, exiting his chest in a spray of blood that spattered and stained the gatepost. He turned for home, walked a few yards, and died.

While the family was grieving for Willie, somebody shot Kels three times with a rifle, from afar, while he was working in his field. The tough old Scotch-Irish pioneer survived, but his arm was shattered, and he would never be the same. While he was in the hospital in Cheyenne, a group of masked riders attacked his sheep herd, running off the new herder and killing many of the animals. The Nickells family, broken at last, would leave their ranch, and take up residence in Cheyenne.

Wyoming had endured almost twenty years of cold and hot range wars between settlers, sheepmen, and big cattle interests. The people were tired of it. The murder of Willie Nickell, far more than the shooting of his father, was written about with outrage in all the major newspapers, and the story became a rallying point for both rage and change. The century had turned, Cheyenne was a burgeoning modern city, and while Tom Horn might be a kind of frontier hero in the saloons, the real Tom Horn was dragging the murderous baggage of the nineteenth century into the industrious and "orderly" twentieth.

He would always say that he never shot Willie Nickell. He testified at the inquest into the boy's killing and seemed sincere in his denial of it; his alibi that he was riding the range about nine miles away was believable. Everybody knew about the Nickell-Miller feud, and knew that Tom Horn was not the only "angel of death" riding the Chugwater country. Horn continued to date Glendolene Kimmell, and to travel widely, to rodeos in Denver, and he went on longer and longer sprees, to cities as far away as Omaha. In Denver, drunk in a bar at four in the morning, he picked a fight with a professional boxer, who broke his jaw and laid him up for three weeks. Sometime during this spree, a drunken Horn also allegedly told saloon patrons that he killed Willie Nickell.

Deputy U.S. Marshal Joe Lefors had known Tom Horn for years. Lefors had also ridden for the Pinkertons, had chased the Wild Bunch, had been a stock detective, though never a hired killer. He was a strange man, with little of the luster of Tom Horn. Lefors was convinced that Horn had killed Willie Nickell, or he was at least convinced that Horn could be convicted of the crime, given his history, reputation, and the fury of the settlers. Taking a cue, perhaps, from Horn's own undercover work, LeFors invented a job in eastern Montana, infiltrating a gang of outlaws who posed as wolfers. LeFors told Horn that he had been asked to find an expert manhunter for a group of wealthy cattlemen who wanted the outlaws killed, and would pay handsomely for the right man. Horn leapt at the chance to go north on such a hunt, just as LeFors knew he would. The two men met in Cheyenne, and Horn, desperate for the fictitious job, began regaling LeFors with tales of his prowess as a stock detective and hired killer. There was plenty of drinking going on, and hidden in a side room was a deputy sheriff and a stenographer. LeFors guided the conversation carefully beyond the issue of the Montana job, and to the Willie Nickell murder. According to the transcript of the conversation, Horn admitted to killing Nickell with his Winchester 1894 .30–30, and walking barefoot to the body to check his shooting, and taking away the spent cartridges. Horn was arrested on January 13, 1902, and charged with the murder.

His friend John Coble paid for his defense. Glendolene Kimmell testified that she was certain that the teenaged Victor Miller had killed Willie Nickell and shot Kels. The drunken confession was widely discredited, though not enough to save Tom Horn. The jury found him guilty. Several of the jurors had known Horn for years. They told newspaper reporters that they liked him, but that the evidence against him was too strong.

While awaiting his appeal, Horn and a fellow inmate overpowered their guard, and fled into the streets of Cheyenne. Horn was recaptured when he could not figure out how to take off the safety of the pistol he had taken, a mistake that saved the life of O. M. Eldrich, a citizen who was chasing him. Eldrich, seeing that Horn could not get the pistol to fire, attacked him and beat him with his own weapon. A crowd took him back to the jail. He spent his days braiding a horsehair rope, writing letters (one to the stenographer, an eloquent plea for him to reconsider his deadly forgery), and hoping for escape or clemency.

Dynamite was found buried in the snow beside the jailhouse walls, an apparent attempt by friends to free him.

Tom Horn went to the gallows on November 20, 1903. He had invited some of his friends to witness his death. Charles Irwin and his brother Frank, at Horn's request, sang a tearful duet of "Life Is Like a Mountain Railroad" as Horn mounted the gallows. Outside the courthouse a crowd of hundreds had gathered to witness the historic death march of one of the West's last heroes, or one of its last untamed men. The crowd included many friends of Tom Horn and was closely watched by a detachment of soldiers. A Gatling gun, manned by an experienced army machine-gunner, was mounted on the roof of the courthouse to discourage any mass attempts to free the condemned man. By the time the hymn was finished, Horn had already helped hangman Joseph Cahill secure the harness and straps around his own body. "You ain't losing your nerve, are you, Joe?" Horn asked Cahill. When the experimental, automated trap turned loose, dropping Tom Horn to a blue-faced death, one of the Old West's most interesting adventurers and killers was gone. He was one day shy of being forty-three years old.

CHAPTER TEN
William "Bill" Tilghman Jr.'s
Colt Single Action Army Revolvers

The Colt Single Action Army Revolver is arguably the most successful hand-gun ever made. The workhorse of the frontier, simple, strong and reliable beyond measure, the Colt Single Action Army was first produced in October of 1873, and called, "The New Model Army Metallic Cartridge Revolving Pistol." The pistol enters history as "The Peacemaker," the "Single Action Army," or "Single Action Frontier." Obviously, the revolver is a single action, meaning that it has to be cocked before firing every one of its six rounds. The action of cocking the pistol also revolves the cylinder, placing the next chamber in

Tilghman carried the other Colt—serial number 235639—during part of his fifty-year career as a lawman.

These Colt Single Action Army Revolvers, .38–40 caliber, are on display at the J. M. Davis Arms and Historical Museum, Claremont, Oklahoma. Both revolvers came to the museum by way of Merle A. Gill, who obtained them from Tilghman through a trade in the early twentieth century.

Courtesy J. M. Davis Arms and Historical Museum, Claremore, Oklahoma

front of the falling firing pin. The cylinder, unlike those of later revolvers, does not swing out from the frame of the weapon for loading. Instead a small loading gate slides aside, exposing the chambers; a simple ejector rod pushes the empty cartridges out, and then the weapon can be reloaded. With the weapon's hammer set at half cock, the cylinder can be rotated freely, and the standard procedure for loading is to load one round, then leave an empty chamber, then load the other four rounds. When the hammer is brought to full cock and then carefully released, it rests on the empty chamber, an absolute necessity, because, if the pistol has one flaw, it is that a blow on the spur of the hammer, which sticks out already to make it handy to the thumb for cocking, can drive the hammer down into the primer of the cartridge below it, firing the weapon. There are dozens if not hundreds of stories of Colt Single Actions falling from holsters, striking the ground, or the floor, and discharging, often with fatal results. The precaution of leaving an empty chamber beneath the hammer was the norm. Many gunfighters, soldiers, and cowboys used the empty chamber to carry a rolled-up $20 bill, to fall back on in hard times, or to cover their own burial expenses.

The design for reloading was created especially for fighters on horseback, the pistol and reins held in the left hand, while the right performs the finer motor skills of ejecting and replacing the cartridges. This was much slower than the swing-out style cylinders of course. However, it contributed to the rocklike durability of the weapon.

The early models came with a 7½- or 5½-inch barrel and were 11 inches long overall.

The first models—and tens of thousands made thereafter—were chambered for the .45 Long Colt, and immediately found favor throughout the world. The .45 Long Colt carried a 250-grain lead bullet backed by thirty-six to forty grains of black powder, all the pressure that the cylinder could handle. With that load the bullet would attain a velocity of about nine hundred feet per second, and strike with the power of a modern .45 ACP, which, as any modern gunfighter can attest, remains the standard for knockdown power in a handgun.

Responding to the popularity of the Model 1873 Winchester Lever Action rifle, which was chambered for the .44-40 metallic cartridge, Colt produced thousands of the "Frontier Model" Army in that caliber. For the first time in history, a person could be armed with a long gun and a handgun, both of them rugged and accurate, and both of them chambered for the same cartridge. The advantages were profound, and the combination soon became one of the most popular weapons systems in the West and would remain so through the 1880s. The revolver was (and still is, for nostalgia buffs and cowboy action shooters, and anyone interested in a rugged beautiful handgun) produced in a dizzying array of other calibers from .32–20 to the European .476 Eley.

The .38–40, as was the case with Bill Tilghman's Colt Army Revolvers, had very similar ballistic performance to the modern .40 Smith & Wesson cartridge, which is one of the most common and effective handgun cartridges of the early twenty-first century. Gun writer and firearms historian Mike Venturino compares the Colt Single Action Army (Colt SAA) with the modern Glock pistol, noting that both weapons are plain, produced in many calibers, and revered for their simplicity, ease of use, accuracy, and most of all, reliability. As the Glock is the handgun of choice of most twenty-first century soldiers and law enforcement officers, so the Colt SAA was to the last quarter of the nineteenth century. It defined the violence in the wildest days of the American Wild West, from Bill Tilghman's expeditions into Indian Territory to Billy the Kid battling his way out of the McSween house during the Lincoln County War, or any of ten thousand bloody altercations along trails and in bars, at poker tables and around campfires, between ex-Confederates and ex-Yankees, sheepmen and cowboys, gold miners, and thieves. The Rough Riders under Teddy Roosevelt charged San Juan Hill in Cuba, firing Colt SAAs at Spanish defenders when they were too close to use their .30–40 Krag rifles. Gen. George Patton killed his first two men with his SAAs, in a skirmish with Pancho Villa's partisans at an isolated hacienda in northern Mexico, during the Mexican Punitive Expedition of 1916. Patton would carry two and use more of the pistols, beautifully engraved and with ivory grips, through his service in World War II. It was the primary sidearm of the closing years of the Plains Indian Wars, used by

Indian and soldier alike. The Colt SAAs issued to Gen. George A. Custer and his troops, which were carried into their defeat at the Battle of Little Bighorn, are believed to still exist, scattered in medicine bundles and secret private collections in homes on the Northern Cheyenne and Pine Ridge Indian Reservations, relics of a triumph in a time of tragedy and loss.

Near Pawnee, Oklahoma, August 1895

It was midafternoon by the time the lawmen found the cabin. All day they had been working their way through the thickets, trying to avoid the trails and scattered Indian camps. They had passed the mouths of narrow canyons where the smell of corn mash and whiskey steam hung like miasma, ridden around a rustler's lair with green cowhides stretched and stinking in the superheated breeze. They were a week's ride from Fort Smith, ready for a week more. The country was hostile, filled with men, women, and even children on the run, and acting as spies for each other from ridge top to creek bottom and back again. The reward for train and bank robber Bill Doolin was up to $5,000, and Doolin was here somewhere, with Bitter Creek Newcomb, Red Buck Waightman, Dynamite Dick Clifton, the whole wild, murdering lot of them, hiding out and recovering from the bloody battle at the Trilby Saloon in Ingalls.

And today, the marshals, Bill Tilghman and Steve Burke, were set to capture two of the most effective spies the Doolin Gang had ever enjoyed. Cattle Annie and Little Britches, wild-haired sirens of the brush country, feral girls in love with bad men, mounted on good stolen horses, Winchesters and Colts in hand, at ease in an anarchic land. When not acting as scouts and spies for the gang, they smuggled their men whiskey and food, dressed wounds, and ferried fresh horses. Cattle Annie, aka Annie McDougal, was seventeen, run off from a homestead farm where she had been the eldest of a mighty brood of children. She got her name from rustling cows, but she liked selling whiskey, too, and stealing horses. Little Britches—Jennie Metcalf—had run off from a hard-up farm, too, after meeting some of the dashing train robbers at a country dance. Little Britches was only fifteen years old. What she lacked in size, she made up for in spit-flying ferocity and skill with guns. Arrested once by veteran marshal Frank Canton for selling whiskey to the Indians, Little Breeches had escaped by stealing Canton's own horse and galloping into the night, back to the lawless country. The outlaw girls were best friends.

Tilghman had taken in many a bad man in his career, had killed Cheyenne warriors in close quarter battle. He and Burke expected to take the girls without a fight. They were still some one hundred yards away when Little Britches suddenly came racing from the cabin's dogtrot and leapt to her horse. She rode straight away, in a thunder of hooves, either to escape or to warn the Doolin Gang of intruders in the territory, or both. Tilghman spurred his horse and gave chase.

Cattle Annie leaned out of the window of the cabin, a rifle in her hands. Burke, creeping along below the windowsill, caught her in a bear hug, and jerked her clear. They went down in a tumble, Cattle Annie clawing for his eyes, Burke trying to get control of the rifle.

Tilghman prided himself on his horses, and he closed with Little Britches on a straightaway run. To his astonishment the diminutive teenager turned in her saddle, drew a revolver, and began to fire at him. Hearing the bullets go by, he slowed a bit, trying to decide what to do. This was no chase to serve a murder warrant, and he refused to do mortal battle with a young girl whose primary crime was her recklessness, a quality that Tilghman himself could not but admire. But she was getting away. Tilghman pulled his Winchester from the saddle scabbard, reined up, and fired a single shot, killing Little Britches's horse. The result was dramatic. The horse pitched forward and rolled, the girl maintaining her seat in the saddle like she was glued there. Horse and rider came to a halt, the horse's hot blood emptying onto the ground in a rush. Little Britches's leg was pinned beneath her mount, and her revolver had been thrown clear of the wreck. Tilghman dismounted, found the gun, and unloaded it, under a withering barrage of curses from the girl. When he kneeled down to lift the horse's weight from her leg, she attacked him, first throwing the double handful of dirt she had been saving in her hands. They wrestled there, in the August heat, the tiny outlaw versus the veteran fighting lawman.

Burke and Tilghman set out for the settlement of Perry, where there was a makeshift jail, Cattle Annie, subdued on her own horse, Little Britches riding in front of Tilghman on his horse. Burke nursed a bloody scratch down the side of his face that stung with sweat. Tilghman, red-eyed and blinking, had dirt still chafing in his eye sockets.

Annie McDougal and Jennie Metcalf were sent to the Framingham Reformatory for Women in Framingham, Massachusetts. According to reports, the two friends treated the train ride east as yet another grand adventure. Neither spent more than eighteen months in Framingham. Reports vary as to their fates; it is believed that Jennie Metcalf went into relief work in the slums of New York, and contracted an illness that killed her a couple of years after her release. Annie McDougal, it is reported, returned to Oklahoma, married, and lived to be 103 years old. She never talked about her two years on the hoot-owl trail with the Doolin Gang.

THE STORY OF BILL TILGHMAN

Bill Tilghman was born on July 4, 1854, at Fort Dodge, Iowa. His father had been a Union soldier and suffered injuries to his eyes, but remained employed by the army as a freighter and sutler, moving his family with the troops along the frontier. Bill Tilghman grew up around the forts, and went to the buffalo hunting grounds when he was fifteen years old, immediately taking his place among some of the West's grittiest hunters and fighters. He would later claim that he killed some seven thousand buffalo during his years on the hunting grounds; his hunting team included his brother Richard, who was killed in one of their many fights with Indians sometime in the 1870s. Tilghman was a scout for the army during the Cheyenne-Arapahoe and the Dull Knife Wars of the mid-1870s, married and settled near Dodge City, Kansas, in 1877, just as that town replaced Abilene as the so-called Queen of the Cow Towns. Tilghman was unsuccessful as a rancher (Indians burned his home and outbuildings in 1879, and his wife and baby narrowly escaped; the cataclysmic winter of 1886–1887 destroyed his herds) but was appointed deputy sheriff by his old friend from the buffalo grounds, Bat Masterson. For the next decade Tilghman would serve as a peace officer, and finally the marshal, in Dodge City, during the three years when the city was known as the wickedest town in the West, earning the respect and friendship of the Earp brothers, Doc Holliday, and a revolving collection of the West's most notorious badmen, cardsharps, con artists, and ladies of the night. Although he also owned and ran two saloons in the city, Tilghman himself did not drink, and maintained a reputation for absolute honesty, a sense of humor, and cool-headedness. A tall, blue-eyed man, weighing no more than 180 pounds, Tilghman was without bluster, and went about his duties in Dodge City with the same good-humored efficiency that had won him respect in the buffalo hunting camps and Indian fights. His early fame as a lawman rested more on his phenomenal ability to establish and maintain the peace than on his willingness to kill. In 1889, when Dodge City became too quiet for him, he took his family and moved south to Guthrie, Oklahoma, to be a part of one of the wildest episodes of American history: the Oklahoma District Land Rush. He made a claim near the settlement of Chandler, and served in various law enforcement jobs in the chaotic new state, never serving long in any one place. He became the chief of police for Oklahoma City in 1892. Upon leaving that job after only a year, Tilghman embarked on the career that would make him famous, as a deputy U.S. marshal hunting outlaws in the Oklahoma and Indian Territories. The job paid about $500 a year, 6 cents a mile for travel, $2 for every warrant served, and whatever the reward was for some of the more prominent outlaws, paid upon conviction. In late 1892 Tilghman was thirty-eight years old, had four children, and his wife Flora was ill with tuberculosis. His home life had long suffered from his work as a lawman, and it was not going to get any better with the new job. The line separating the Oklahoma Territory and what was left of the Indian Territories was called Hell's Fringe. Beyond it, the country teemed with outlaws and rogues drawn to the sanctuary of lawlessness. For Tilghman, perhaps, the paltry wages meant nothing. Wearing a badge, outfitted with a fine horse, a Winchester rifle, and a pair of Colt Single Action Army Revolvers, it must have seemed like a kind of hunter's paradise.

Bill Tilghman as he looked while acting as the Marshal of Dodge City, during the time when it was the "wickedest city in the West." In Dodge City he would meet and befriend men like the Earp brothers and Doc Holliday, among many others, who were drawn to his easy-going, no-nonsense, and deadly serious manner of enforcing the law.

Courtesy Robert G. McCubbin Collection

The marshals he joined were a mixed bunch, many of them not much better than the outlaws they pursued; others were decent, law-honoring men. A handful were professionals like Tilghman. For all of them, it was a warrior's life, with manhunts covering a thousand miles, and months on the trail, all of it in hostile country, with the need for secrecy and undercover work always paramount. Of the two hundred marshals who rode for the federal court at Fort Smith, Arkansas, sixty-five would die in gunfights. When Tilghman began his work, the Dalton Gang had just met disaster at Coffeyville, Kansas, when they robbed two banks at once on an October day in 1892. In the wild street fight that followed, three of the town's civilian defenders and a U.S. marshal were killed. But four out of five of the Dalton Gang were shot dead in the streets, and the lone survivor, Emmett Dalton, collapsed at the edge of town after having been shot an astounding twenty-three times.

The Doolin Gang would soon take up any slack created by the fast-shooting citizens of Coffeyville.

Tilghman joined marshals Chris Madsen and Heck Thomas in pursuit of the Doolin Gang. The three lawmen would go down in history as the Three Guardsmen. They were lawmen of a type never quite seen before or since. Heck Thomas had been a Confederate cavalry soldier in the Civil War, and then the marshal of bloody Fort Worth, Texas. He had been riding for the court of "Hanging Judge" Isaac Parker since 1875, serving warrants and bringing in fugitives throughout the Indian Territories. Chris Madsen was born in Denmark and served in the Danish Army in the war against the Prussians in 1864. He spent years with the French Foreign Legion before coming to the United States in the early 1870s. Following his chosen profession, he eventually became a chief of scouts for the U.S. Army in the campaigns against the Apache, the Sioux, the Cheyenne, and the Nez Percé. Madsen came to work for the U.S. marshals in 1891, the year before Tilghman began.

Against such men the Doolin Gang was doomed. Tilghman, working alone, trailed leader Bill Doolin to Eureka Springs, Arkansas, where the outlaw was using the healing waters on his multiple nagging bullet wounds, and captured him without firing a shot. He would never collect the reward, however;

One of the marble tablets at the Oklahoma Law Enforcement Memorial in Oklahoma City features Tilghman's likeness, one of the "Three Guardsmen," along with various firearms used by law enforcement throughout the years.
Courtesy Oklahoma Law Enforcement Memorial, Inc.

Doolin escaped from jail before his trial, and then was killed by Heck Thomas in the summer of 1896. Madsen killed gang members Dynamite Dick Clifton, Little Dick West, and the homicidal wildman Red Buck Waightman. Tilghman shot Little Bill Raidler, captured him, and then helped him get a parole from prison because his wounds were so debilitating. Over a decade the Three Guardsmen captured over three hundred fugitives and outlaws in the Indian Territories, and are widely considered responsible for breaking the long-standing power of outlawry in the region.

Heck Thomas retired in 1909; Madsen served as a lawman, in an administrative capacity, until 1922. But Tilghman, even though he took time out for his horse breeding and movie making (he made and promoted two movies, *The Bank Robber* and *The Passing of the Oklahoma Outlaws,* and one of his horses won the Kentucky Derby), stayed very much in the saddle as a lawman.

His first wife died in 1900, and in 1903 he married again, to Zoe Stratton, a twenty-two-year-old woman from the town of Ingalls, once the headquarters of the Doolin Gang. President Teddy Roosevelt personally sent him to Mexico to track down a runaway embezzler. In 1910 he was elected to the Oklahoma Senate, but apparently could not stand the job; he resigned after one year to become chief of police in Oklahoma City, his second time in that job. In 1924 the governor of Oklahoma asked Tilghman to take on the job of bringing order to the oil-boom city of Cromwell. It was a job akin to cleaning out the Augean Stables, against which even Tilghman's days in Dodge City must have seemed relatively quaint. A new order prevailed in Cromwell, organized crime, providing every imaginable vice to cash-heavy oil-field workers drawn from all corners of the nation. By all accounts the town was a snake pit, an oil-soaked hell where killings were so common that no one even retrieved the bodies, where naked prostitutes were on display in illegal speakeasies, and drugs like cocaine and heroin were as available as illegal alcohol. The forces of order were there—lawmen and prohibition agents—but they had been corrupted by the amount of money to be made. Tilghman came into town a seventy-year-old-man, reportedly suffering from advanced cancer. By all accounts he made headway in cleaning up the town, using the same steady, bluster-free iron hand that had served him so well as a youth in Dodge City. And by some accounts, there was a price on his head because of it. On Halloween night, 1924, Tilghman stepped outside Ma Murphy's Cafe on Cromwell's main street, to investigate someone shooting a handgun. Wiley Lynn, a corrupt prohibition agent, was reeling drunk, pistol in hand, in the company of some local prostitutes and their clients. Tilghman drew his own pistol, a .32 automatic, and snatched the pistol away from Lynn with his left hand. Trying to calm the prohibition officer down, Tilghman stepped close to him, only to be shot twice in the chest when Lynn reached another pistol that he had hidden in his coat pocket. Tilghman had survived being shot at least four times in his long career, but he would not survive this time.

His body lay in state in the Oklahoma State Capitol Building in Oklahoma City for three days before being buried. Tilghman's cousin, G. Wayne

Tilghman, who has written a book about the lawman's life, writes that Bat Masterson concluded the eulogies for Tilghman's long and eventful life, saying simply, "He was the greatest of us all."

A month after the funeral, someone—perhaps an old friend of Tilghman's—set fire to the business and red-light districts of Cromwell and burned them flat.

CHAPTER ELEVEN
Pancho Villa's Smith & Wesson
Model 3 American Revolver

Celaya, Guanajuato, Mexico, April 13, 1915—these dandies were tricky indeed. They were fighting some other kind of war now, it seemed, with tactics they must have learned from their fellow degenerate *perfumados* on the battlefields of Europe. How fitting, and how disgusting, that these vessels of tea-sipping corruption would import such cowardly methods of warfare to Mexico, and then try to bring them to bear on the great Division of the North, the proud horsemen of the desert, simple men who had never owned anything, but who had broken the chokehold of the soft-handed tyrants, fey

The Smith & Wesson Model 3 American Revolver believed to be carried by Mexican revolutionary commander Doroteo Arango, aka Pancho Villa, and used in the Mexican Revolution and the subsequent Mexican Civil War, is a single action, six-shot, .44 caliber weapon, with an 8-inch barrel. On display at the J. S. Adams Arms Museum, Claremore, Oklahoma, it had been purchased by Merle A. Gill from former "Villista" Pablo González, in El Paso, Texas, in 1933.

Courtesy J. M. Davis Arms and Historical Museum, Claremore, Oklahoma

and murderous, who had held their nation in bondage for centuries. Now the tyrannical dandies were back, in the guise of fellow revolutionary Alvaro Obregón, who seemed appalled that such simple men could actually expect to share power with him.

It started in 1910 as a righteous revolution of serfs and peasants against a decadent class of rulers that had dominated Mexico through thuggery, and bled its wealth for generations. Within three years, the revolution had metastasized into a civil war and anarchy that convulsed the nation. The Four Horsemen of the Apocalypse galloped unfettered though city and country-side alike. By the time the fighting sputtered to an exhausted halt in the 1920s, estimates of the dead range above one million souls, with perhaps 250,000 of those active combatants. Some believe that as many as three million people died, from warfare, murder, starvation, and the series of diseases, among them the Spanish Flu, that devastated weary armies and the terrorized civilians that fled them.

Francisco "Pancho" Villa, the great Centaur of the North, wheeled his warhorse Siete Leguas and charged, yet again. His elite cavalry, Los Dora-dos, once five hundred strong, were chewed down to a couple hundred exhausted and wounded souls. Yet still they followed him, the dust rising around them in stiff clouds, the clear light of the Mexican highlands glistening on the silver coils of razor wire scattered everywhere before the trenches that sheltered his enemies. Siete Leguas surged forward, high stepping through the coils of wire, leaping the shattered carcasses of yesterday's charges, the horses stretched and stiff in their death agonies, men pinned beneath them. Once these men were goatherds, field hands, serfs to the rich. Villa had made them horsemen and warriors, freemen of the first caliber. And that is how they had died; their clothes black with dried blood, their bodies shot to ribbons in the cross fire of the Hotchkiss seven-millimeter machine guns. Villa fired at a tall Yaqui Indian who was working the bolt on his Mauser 98, and the man tumbled down the bank of the irrigation ditch. But the Hotchkiss guns were opening up again as Villa and the Dorados closed in. Obregón's fighters were sheltering like women in the ditches, but they were laying down a crushing fire. Bullets buzzed and sizzled, whacked into the flesh of men and horses, thudded into the leather of boots and saddles, clanged on rifles and pistols. From the plains behind the ditches, the dreaded Mondragon guns began firing like a monstrous and steady heartbeat. The crazy-house shriek of seventy-five-millimeter artillery shells drowned the noise of the fighting for a brief second, and then the earth seemed to open and vomit up men and horses.

The charge broke. Villa, his famous bloodlust courage still upon him, leapt the ditch, his Winchester empty, firing his Smith & Wesson revolver down into the Yaqui troops crouching there. At a dead gallop he broke the revolver open and reloaded, coming at the troops from behind their own lines, setting the front sight on the backs of men scrambling to escape, at the chests of men calmly leveling their Mausers at him. As if from far away, he could hear the Hotchkiss guns thunder, the crackling of the Mauser enfilade, and he noticed that the crack! crack! crack! of the .30–30s favored by his Dorados was slowing to silence. He spurred hard, back across the lines, over the mounds of thrashing horses and broken men that now covered the worst of the razor wire. The stink of ruptured entrails and dung, cordite, and gun smoke was in his nose, spatters of blood and brain on his leggings. He fired his revolver into the air, and joined the rout, what was left of his greatest men galloping north in tiny bands, colliding with each other and with enemy riders, a melee of gunfire and pistol fights in dust too thick to determine friend or foe. Behind him, there was a slowly building roar from the defenders, a tinny bugle ringing in triumph. Behind him, four thousand men of his Division of the North lay piled in shattered heaps, never again to see the mountains of Chihuahua, or dance with the beautiful girls of Coahuila. Eight thousand more were throwing away their weapons and waiting for their captors. The war would go on for four more long years, but after this day of blood and madness, Pancho Villa, who rose from surly farmhand to bandit to one of the world's most powerful military leaders, was once more a mere bandit king.

THE STORY OF THE SMITH & WESSON MODEL 3 REVOLVER

The Smith & Wesson Model 3 Revolver was first introduced in 1870, and was the world's first reliable "top-break" revolver, meaning that the barrel and cylinder could be released and swung forward, barrel down, exposing the six chambers in the cylinder for rapid reloading. The Model 3s—and there were a lot of them, in various designs, almost 250,000 before production ceased in 1912—all have the characteristic round hinge just below and in front of the cylinder.

The Model 3s were an almost immediate success, and Smith & Wesson's first real challenge to the dominance of the Colt in the American West. It was the world's first "big bore" (.44 caliber) revolver chambered for a metallic cartridge rather than cap and ball (S & W had been producing .32 and .22 rimfire, metallic-cartridge revolvers all through the Civil War. These were extremely low-powered weapons compared with the cap-and-ball .36s and .44s in common use). The first Model 3s, released in 1870, were chambered for the Henry .44 Rimfire, the same chambering as the Winchester Model 1866 Lever Action, perhaps to capitalize on the concept of being able to carry one kind of ammo for both rifle and pistol. But the .44 Henry Rimfire cartridge, for all the success of the famous Winchester lever gun that fired it, was always recognized as underpowered. There were concerns that a beefier cartridge than the .44 Rimfire would prove too much for the top-break design of the Model 3, but the demands of the market soon pushed Smith & Wesson to look for a better cartridge anyway. The Civil War was over, but the Indian Wars were at their peak, and the U.S. Army was actively looking for a new sidearm design that could carry a round with true knockdown power. Army armorers liked what they saw in the design of the top-break Model 3, but they refused to purchase the revolvers in a rimfire cartridge, especially not the .44 Henry, which the army had never trusted. The answer was the .44 S & W American. Ballistically, it was no big step up from the .44 Henry—there were still concerns about the pistol blowing up from a too-powerful cartridge—but it was centerfire, and at first, it was bigger than anything else out there in a revolver. Loaded up—it was the first metallic cartridge designed to be reloaded—it could drive a 200-grain lead bullet a respectable 750 feet per second. The competition, introduced in 1873, was the slow-to-reload Colt Single Action Army in .45—the army's standard issue sidearm at the time. The Colt SAA threw a 250-grain bullet at nine hundred feet per second, but its simple mechanics are renowned for strength. The S & W Model 3s in .44 American gave up a little bit in power, added a bit of unwanted complexity, but gained much in speed and ease of reloading. The U.S. Army liked what it saw and made an initial purchase of one thousand Model 3s. At least four of these eventually made it to the Battle of the Little Bighorn, judging by shell casings found there by archeologists. It is unknown who used them there, but one thing is certain, after that battle at least four proud Indian warriors were carrying the most advanced handgun of the day into new conflicts.

The Model 3s would evolve quickly over the years. The revolver was chambered for the new .44 Russian cartridge in 1871, in response to an order from the Russian Army. Grand Duke Alexis came to America to make the deal, and to watch the production of this new sidearm for his troops. While in America the Grand Duke was guided on a long buffalo hunt by Buffalo Bill Cody, and accompanied in the field by Gen. Phil Sheridan and Gen. George Armstrong Custer. Cody was already carrying and using the Model 3s in his expeditions on the plains, and Alexis was said to have marveled at Cody's skill with the new guns. When Alexis tried to bring down a buffalo with his own custom-made Model 3s—an engraved set of pistols presented to him by Smith & Wesson and valued at over $400, an astronomical sum at the time—the animal soaked up all of the .44 Russian rounds and kept lumbering away over the horizon.

Smith & Wesson produced the Model 3, in many variations and calibers, until 1912. It proved to be a favorite of outlaws and lawmen alike. Jesse James carried one, the Model 3 Schofield, in .45 S & W; his murderer, Bob Ford, used the .44. Pat Garrett is said to have owned one, as did John Wesley Hardin, at some point in his furious career. The popularity of the guns was neck and neck with the Colt Single Action Army Model 1873.

Where Pancho Villa obtained his Model 3 will never be known (he captured, literally, tens of thousands of rifles, pistols, and artillery pieces during his years as a bandit and as a military commander), but it may have had some sentimental value to him, because by 1917, when he allegedly sold or gave it to Pablo González, the Colt 1911, .45 ACP, semiautomatic was already king of the battlefield, and yet he had held on to this beautiful old revolver. Villa's love for fine guns was legendary, and after his assassination, his widow, Señora Luz Corral de Villa, sold many weapons that were alleged to have belonged to him, and probably quite a few that never did, to help support the house full of children, none of them hers, that Villa fathered with his estimated twenty-four other wives. Señora Luz Corral died in 1980.

THE STORY OF PANCHO VILLA

Villa began his life as Doroteo Arango. His father died when he was fifteen, leaving him the eldest son and sole supporter of his family. They were not peons, but sharecroppers, living in a nation where seventeen of the richest families—the grandest *hacendados*—owned 150,000 square miles of agricultural and grazing lands. For the multitudes of landless, there was only servitude, and for the insubordinate, there was only death. In September of 1894 when Doroteo was sixteen years old, he shot the *hacendado* for whom he worked, for molesting his little sister. He took to the wild mountains of Durango, the last redoubt of the men and women, many of them Indians, who refused to live a life of slavery and poverty. When he was captured by the *rurales,* men who were given weapons and free reign to terrorize and rob the people in return for their absolute loyalty to Mexico's dictator, Porfirio Díaz, the *rurales* made him grind the corn for their tortillas, while transporting him to his execution. Doroteo used the grinder, a heavy stone called a *metate,* to kill one of his captors, and escape back into the wilds.

He took up residence in the Sierra De La Silla, fought off the *rurales* again and again, killing men and horses. He became a member of a bandit gang that roamed throughout Chihuahua, raiding the mule trains that supplied the mines where men worked long days for almost nothing. The bandits stole payrolls, horses, cattle. In 1896 Doroteo was wounded in a furious gunfight with *rurales.* Somewhere in that time he renamed himself Francisco "Pancho" Villa. The new man tried to go straight, running a butcher shop, even working in the mines, but he had a price on his head, and anyway, under the thumb of Díaz and his cronies, the nation of Mexico lay in torpor, its riches siphoned away, its people kept landless and poor to provide labor for the *hacendados,* the mines, lumber mills, the new petroleum fields. The country, once a rich agricultural land, could not even feed itself because the *hacendados* managed their lands so poorly. Most food was imported. Only the rich could afford it. The poor ate what they could find, or starved, all the while looking at millions of acres of unused farmland from which they were barred. They owned nothing, and they were laughed at if they tried to borrow money from the banks. When Villa and a friend tried to start a new butcher shop, they found that two families controlled all the slaughtering facilities in Chihuahua. If you wanted to sell beef, you had to get it from them, at prices so high that you could not make a profit.

Villa's frustration was mirrored, a million times over, across Mexico. As always, real unrest began with the educated, entrepreneurial classes who found themselves locked out of the business and political structure of their own country. These were young people who had lived in the United States and Europe; they knew that there were other ways of running a nation. By 1910 frustration turned to fury. Villa, back on the bandit trail, hunted by *rurales* and federal troops, had a ballooning reputation as a folk hero, a man who attacked the oppressors and helped the oppressed, and who could not be taken down. He was invited to join the revolution, and he did.

The rest is a kind of hyperviolent fairy tale. Villa would learn to read and write, but he would never get over his distrust of those who already knew how. He pursued a course of banditry against the government, but on a grand scale, with thousands of irregular troops behind him, and he expanded the concept of banditry to include taking whole cities, and expropriating loans for the revolution from the families who had once ruled the land with

Gen. Pancho Villa.

1391-S

U.S. history books call him a bandit, Mexican history books call him one of their nation's revolutionary heroes. In reality, Pancho Villa was both. While some bandits robbed the passengers of trains, Pancho Villa took the trains themselves, mounted heavy weaponry upon them, loaded them with troops, and used them to assault and take entire towns. While some bandits stole money from banks, Villa took over the banks themselves, printed his own currency, and tried to use the money to help his impoverished country.

absolute power. Instead of robbing trains, he took them whole, mounted artillery upon them, and used them to attack more cities. His reputation for honesty was matched by one for terror. His sobriety was unique among bandits and military men alike. It gave him a terrifying edge, as if combat, wariness, and the rush of violence were the only drugs he required. Except for his satyr-like love of women, which only added to his fame as a true man of Mexico, the irrepressible macho, so long beat down by tyranny, now free to express his true nature, relaxing with the ladies after a day of dust and blood and challenge.

Porfirio Díaz fled Mexico. One of the last and most decisive battles of his regime took place in 1911, in Juarez, just across the border from El Paso. Americans in El Paso stood on top of boxcars in the train yard and watched as Villa's army smashed the federal troops in heavy fighting. Francisco Madero, the choice of the revolutionaries for president, took the reins. But Mexico was a runaway bronco, bucking and pitching in what looked like a suicidal frenzy. Rebellion and betrayal were the order of the day, and violent pillage was the actual master. Madero lost power and was murdered. Villa himself was imprisoned in Mexico City for insubordination and sentenced to the firing squad by his comrade in arms, Gen. Victoriano Huerta. Villa escaped and returned to his troops in the north. By 1914 he was in command of almost twenty thousand men, and fighting was continuous. His tactics were straightforward, with little room for complex strategy or nuance. He asked for the surrender of cities, and if the federal troops defending them did not comply, he laid siege to them, with tremendous artillery barrages followed by cavalry charges. It was a meat-grinder approach. Casualties on all sides, and among civilians, were always very high. But the Division of the North, as it came to be called, was a modern army, with fleets of ambulances, field hospitals, troop trains, and excellent weapons. After each victory Villa offered defeated troops the option of joining his forces, with eloquent appeals to patriotism and the future of the oppressed. His ranks swelled to forty thousand men, all of them relatively well supplied and paid a peso a day. American soldiers of fortune, and American medical staff, could make money in the conflict, which was just down the road

*The backbone of the Division del Norte, Pancho Villa and his most trusted lieutenants, men
of the country, hardened by the deserts and mountains of Chihuahua, Sonora, Coahuila.
Shut out by a decadent political system, they called Villa the great Centaur of the North,
and rallied behind him, hungry for battle, for plunder, for justice.*
Library of Congress, LC-DIG-ggbain-29882

from Texas and New Mexico. Many of them enlisted. American arms deal-
ers made fortunes. After spectacular fights at Chihuahua City and Ojinaga,
Pancho Villa, once Doroteo Aranga a man of the fields and a bandit, became
governor of Chihuahua, a land larger than Great Britain.

Pancho Villa seems to have been a man of intelligence, charisma, and
ferocity, but he was never a politician. His happiest days seem to have been
in battle, or in the encampments in the deserts and mountains of northern
Mexico. When he brought his army to Mexico City, the complex internecine
struggles of the revolution overwhelmed him. Perhaps he could not reconcile
the ideals of the revolution, or the purity of combat, with the sleazier struggle
for the power that would be needed to actually change the nation. He despised

Mexico's new leader Venustiano Carranza, and he refused to serve him, or the commander of Carranza's troops, Alvaro Obregón. They seemed to him to be exactly what he had been fighting all his life, *los perfumados,* corrupt and egotistical dandies, would-be dictators with no concern for the working poor who had given them the revolution. Villa rebelled.

He was far from home, on Mexico's high central plateau, a colder world, intensely settled for centuries, with none of the wild sanctuaries of his native Chihuahua. He brought his division, and Los Dorados, his elite cavalry strike force, against Obregón's troops at a town called Celaya. Obregón was from Sonora, and was not really the *perfumado* that Villa considered him. He had a large number of Yaqui Indian troops, to whom he had promised the return of their ancestral lands in Sonora. They were fierce warriors, and had been for centuries. Obregón had been obsessively reading about and studying the battles of World War I, then raging across the Atlantic, with its modern trench warfare, placement of artillery, interlocking fields of heavy machine gun fire, miles of razor wire, all the murderous new techniques of a murderous age. He applied as many as he could, using a grid of irrigation ditches for trenches. On a smaller scale, he had all the same weaponry that his European counterparts had, and he set them up in the most modern tactical configurations. When Villa attacked him, with his primitive lightning charges, it was a disaster for the Division of the North. It was the beginning of the end. Villa returned to Chihuahua, pursued by Obregón. The United States had always been a Villa ally; suddenly, President Woodrow Wilson threw his support behind Carranza. Villa saw this as proof that the powers of the world were allied against ever letting the poor rise up. The Division of the North, what was left of it, lacked cohesion. Banditry became common again, committed against a war-weary and pillaged land. Supplies and ammunition ran scarce. The working people of the country were in worse shape than ever. A band of Villistas murdered seventeen American mining engineers during a train robbery in Chihuahua. American cowboys working for an American-owned ranch in Mexico, whose owners had always been friendly with Villa, were hanged. Then, on March 8, 1916, Villa led several hundred of his men north of the border and struck the American town of Columbus, New Mexico. A surprised U.S. Army garrison fought back in a battle at close quarters. A Villista was killed with a baseball bat; others were scalded with boiling water. The fighting spilled through the little town, with Villa and his men desperately trying to grab military supplies even as the town began to burn. Eight American soldiers and ten civilians were killed. The Villistas escaped with a haul of pack and riding horses and mules, a load of three hundred Mauser 98s, and ammunition. The American soldiers pursued them, and killed at least seventy-five of the raiders. It was a far cry from the taking of Zacatecas.

American general John "Black Jack" (so named because he had once commanded a regiment of black soldiers) Pershing was given the task of destroying Pancho Villa. Pershing had last seen Chihuahua as a young lieutenant, in pursuit of Geronimo and his Apache raiders. Now, some thirty years later, Pershing led the Mexican Punitive Expedition, a force of almost six thousand troops, into the same harsh country. The expedition was doomed by top-heaviness. Horses lacked forage in the deserts; the men lacked experience in high mountains where the temperatures ranged between ninety degrees at noon and below freezing at night. Before the end of March, heavy mountain snows tortured the troops.

> "He always impressed me as a man of great force and energy and willing to do right when directed by those he respected. After all, he was a poor peon without any advantages in his youth, persecuted and pursued through the mountains, his life always in danger; but he had the cause of the poor peon at heart. He was fully aware of his own deficiencies and even at the height of his power had no desire for the presidency."
>
> —HUGH L. SCOTT, CHIEF OF STAFF OF THE U.S. ARMY, 1914–1917, QUOTED IN RONALD ATKIN'S REVOLUTION

Close calls with armed and infuriated Mexicans became common, although the Villistas remained hidden. On May 5, at a place called Blue Springs, an American force, accompanied by Apache scouts, came upon a large body of Villa's troops. The fighting was intense, accounting for forty-four Villistas killed. The rest of May seemed like a turning point for the Americans. A young lieutenant, George S. Patton, out driving with a tiny group of soldiers to buy supplies, would engage with, and kill, Villa's top commander of the Dorados, Gen. Julio Cardenas, in a dramatic pistol battle. Patton killed two of the general's men in the same fight. The triumphant Americans purchased their supplies and rode back to camp with the bodies of the Mexicans on the hood of the car.

The expedition eventually ran afoul of deadly politics when a hot-headed young American commander got into a battle with a Mexican general and his troops, with many casualties on both sides. The Punitive Expedition found itself restrained after that. Villa, knowing that he was no longer in danger from them, began to raid in earnest. By January of 1917, Pershing led his troops back to the United States. The expedition was estimated to have cost about $130 million, and was widely seen as a fiasco.

Villa would eventually make peace with Carranza and his government in 1920. Carranza gave Villa a twenty-five-thousand-acre estate called El Canutillo, in excellent ranching and farming country in Chihuahua. Fifty or more of the Dorados settled on the estate as bodyguards, and brought their families to live there. El Canutillo became, in microcosm, a model of what Villa had once hoped that Mexico could become. He operated a bank that offered credit to farmers and sold goods in stores for wholesale prices. Some of Villa's estimated twenty-three wives settled there, and some of his many children. He was a fiend for education, and he set up one of the world's first literacy campaigns at El Canutillo. Bulky and intent, the Commander of the Division of the North, conqueror of Zacatecas, sat in his desk in the classroom with the children of peasants, learning to read and do mathematics. He was renowned for his love of and respect for children. One can easily imagine him instructing his sons, letting them practice with his beloved revolver, telling them tales of glorious battle and the pursuit of justice, perhaps leaving out the banditry, perhaps not.

Then, on July 20, 1923, while on a trip to the nearby town of Parral, Pancho Villa was assassinated by a team of seven gunmen who opened fire on his car.

CHAPTER TWELVE
Frank Hamer's Remington Model 8 Semi-Auto

The Remington Model 8 would have been a Winchester, if genius gun designer John Browning had not had a falling out with Winchester vice president Thomas Gray Bennett, early in 1902, when he was first trying to produce his new design for a civilian version of a semiautomatic rifle. It also could have been a Fabrique Nationale, manufactured in Belgium, if import tariffs had not impeded that deal. Browning, the Ogden, Utah–born son of a Mormon pioneer and gunsmith, was the creator of the world's most perfect handgun design—the Colt 1911—and arguably the second most popular handgun on earth until the 1990s, the Browning Hi-Power, Browning's last work before he died. As it turned out, John Browning took his patent for his auto-loading rifle to Remington, and they began producing the Model 8 in 1906. Between then and when it ceased production in 1936 (a variation, the Model 81 Woodsmaster, familiar to many a deer hunter, would continue until

This Remington Model 8 .30 Caliber Semi-Auto was presented to Texas Ranger Frank Hamer by the Remington Arms Company in 1922. Hamer gained fame as the leader of the ambush that killed Bonnie Parker and Clyde Barrow. His Remington is exhibited in the Texas Ranger Museum, Waco, Texas.

Courtesy of: Sam Houston Sanders Corps of Cadets Center, College Station, TX

1950), the Remington Arms Company produced 80,600 of them, in calibers .25, .30, and .35 Remington. It was a favorite of law enforcement officers, who were increasingly finding themselves outgunned by outlaws from the turn of the century through the Great Depression.

The Remington Model 8 was a recoil-operated autoloader—not a machine gun—that required the shooter to pull the trigger each time it was fired. Its design was based on the revolutionary Browning long recoil action, perfected by John Browning in 1900, and used in the famous Browning A-5 shotguns. The recoil from the exploding cartridge is used to operate the loading mechanism. The downside of the design was its weight and bulk—the Model 8 weighed nine pounds on average.

The Story of Frank Hamer

Texas Ranger captain Frank Hamer was among the most ferocious and dogged lawmen of any age, in any nation. In a fifty-year-long career as a peace officer of sorts along the Texas–Mexico border, Hamer would be involved in nearly one hundred gunfights, shot twenty-three times, and kill fifty-three men, his opponents ranging from ruthless Mexican bandits and smugglers, to professional assassins, swindlers, and car theft ringleaders, to the reckless and mythical gunner Clyde Barrow and his lover, Bonnie Parker. Frank Hamer grew up around San Saba County, Texas, and was a hunter and woods-wanderer as a boy, enamored of the lives and habits of the Tonkawas and Apaches and other tribes that had lived and fought in the same hills that his family called home. He would become famous as a tracker of men, a unique detective who effectively bridged the lawless horse-born outlaw days and the urban, machine guns and fast cars of the Public Enemy Era of the Depression and beyond.

His youth ended early. Hamer and his brother Harrison were share-cropping a San Saba farm owned by Dan McSwain, who offered Frank $150 to kill a neighbor with whom he'd been having a dispute. Frank's refusal, and the fact that he told the neighbor of the threat, infuriated McSwain, who

Frank Hamer killed his first man at age sixteen, almost fell in with an outlaw gang led by Black Jack Ketcham, but turned instead to the job of law enforcement, a job he would hold for fifty years. That job would involve approximately one hundred gunfights, twenty-three gunshot wounds, and fifty-three men killed. According to Hamer biographers John H. Jenkins and H. Gordon Frost, this portrait photo was taken the day after Hamer had killed the murderous Ed Putnam in a gunfight in 1906 near Del Rio, Texas. Hamer would have been twenty-two years old.

Courtesy of the Texas Ranger Hall of Fame and Museum, Waco, TX

tried to kill him with a shotgun, failing only because Harrison screamed out a warning. Frank was struck by a load of buckshot, some of which he would carry all his life, but he managed to return fire with his pistol, one of the bullets knocking McSwain to the ground. McSwain survived, and Frank Hamer left the country to recover from wounds to his back and head, camping and hunting alone along the Pecos River. When he felt strong enough, he rode back to McSwain's farm and killed him. Frank was sixteen years old. His brother Harrison was twelve. Hamer would stay on the side of the law the rest of his life, despite the siren call of outlawry (his first job as a cowhand was working for the brother of the notorious robber and gang leader Black Jack Ketchum), and Hamer himself, at nineteen, once rode into San Angelo to rob the bank there, only to have his cowhand work interfere and despite the fact that the powers he represented as a lawman sometimes seemed equally corrupt and destructive. In fact, when Hamer was an old man, at the end of a violent career, he would say that his most difficult and unpleasant struggles had always been with corrupt men in positions of authority. In 1915, at the midpoint of the Mexican Revolution (a war that killed an estimated one out of every fifteen Mexicans before it ended in 1921), an order came down to the Texas Rangers from the state government in Austin to ignore the embargo on arms flowing across the border to the bandits and revolutionaries who were using northern Mexico as a staging area for attacks far and wide, on Texans and Mexicans alike. Hamer knew the embargo had been put in place by President Woodrow Wilson, and that his men, and the citizens he was charged with protecting, would be the targets of any guns that flowed across the border. The order was obviously the result of a bribe, or someone in state government with an interest in arms sales. Hamer ignored it, and kept up his hunt for arms smugglers. Slowly, he realized that a greater power was at work. One by one his fellow Rangers were reassigned to duty in other parts of Texas. Finally, only Hamer remained, patrolling hundreds of miles of rough country in the midst of a war, and in a place where Rangers had fought and killed hundreds of bandits since he'd begun work. Instead of leaving his post, he simply rode across

Shortly after he was married in 1917, Hamer became the target of a group of hired assassins in Johnson County, Texas, when working with the Texas Cattle Raiser's Association, to eliminate the last of the cattle rustlers operating around the state. In the course of that work, he was drawn into an investigation of a land dispute that had led to at least one murder. Harrison Hamer, Frank's brother, who was working in the area as a cowboy, also became a target of the killers. Frank and Harrison hunted down the assassins, found two of them on the street in Snyder, Texas, and challenged them to a gunfight. Caught off-guard, the men would not draw their pistols. Harrison and Frank each took one of them, and in Harrison's words, "stomped hell out of them." It might have offered satisfaction, but it solved nothing. Hamer went on to testify at the murder trial, then found himself, with his wife, Gladys, and Harrison, caught in an ambush on the street in Sweetwater, Texas. Frank was shot twice, with a .45, at point blank range, before disarming his first attacker, who then ran to a car and rearmed himself. Gladys Hamer saw another assassin, armed with a shotgun, coming for Frank from behind. The new bride grabbed her handgun and began to fire at the man, forcing him to take cover behind a parked car. When Gladys ran out of ammunition, the assassin closed the distance to Frank fast, and shot from three feet, missing his head but blowing off his hat brim. The fight ended with the shotgunner running for his life and the first attacker dead.

After a short hospital stay, Frank recovered from his wounds by taking a long driving trip with Gladys, traveling through the West and enjoying a long stay at Yellowstone National Park.

the Rio Grande and joined with a force of Mexican *rurales,* who had been locked in a death match with Pancho Villa and his fighters. They eagerly accepted Hamer into their group, and together they patrolled both sides of the border, fighting and intercepting arms and stolen horses, until whoever made the chaos gave up.

In 1917 Prohibition gave rise to a new frenzy of smuggling along the border. Hard-living Rangers like Frank Hamer probably thought that Prohibition was ridiculous, but they enforced it as the law of the land. With the smuggling, as it always does, came an epidemic of lawlessness. As recorded in his remarkable biography, *I'm Frank Hamer,* Hamer would tell his son Frank Jr. of those days in El Paso, that somewhere in the town, "There was a gunfight for 236 straight nights." A 1918 border ambush of a group of hard-core Mexican smugglers led by desperado Incarnacíon Delgado might have been a turning point for Hamer in his understanding of how to deal with truly dangerous men. Cameron County Sheriff W. T. Vann was determined to take Delgado prisoner, if possible, without a fight. Hamer knew that this was impossible. Armed with his now favorite rifle, the Remington Model 8—this one was believed to be a .25 caliber—and "Old Lucky," Hamer reluctantly bowed to the commands of the sheriff.

The ambush went just as Hamer had predicted. When Vann called out for the smugglers to surrender, Delgado opened fire, felling Ranger Delbert Timberlake with a gruesome stomach wound that would kill him before the night was out. Hamer bore down with the Remington Model 8, firing at the place where the muzzle flashes had appeared in the thickets. To the Rangers and deputies hidden near him, the rifle was firing so fast that it looked like one of the propane torches that ranchers used to burn the spines off prickly pears, so that hungry cattle and goats could feed on them. "Good God," one of the men said, "Look at Frank use that pear burner on him!" Delgado was killed instantly. The Remington Arms Company would present Hamer with an engraved Model 8, featuring scenes from some of his most famous battles, in 1922. Ironically, his most famous battles, and his record-breaking numbers of successful cases, were still ahead of him at that time. And it would be far into a violent and controversial future—not until 1934—that Texas Prison's manager Lee Simmons would send him after Clyde Barrow. Frank Hamer brought everything he had learned to that chase. After inspecting a shot-to-pieces getaway car, another of the famous Ford V8s that the Barrow gang used—stole—exclusively, Hamer noted that, of thirty rounds fired into the car by a .45 Thompson machine gun wielded by a lawman, seventeen had connected. None of them had penetrated into the car. He went to Austin, to Jake Petmecky's gun shop, and ordered a new "pear burner" Remington Model 8, this time in .35 Remington, the largest caliber available, and he had it fitted with a twenty-pound, police-only magazine. The rifle was heavy, and fully loaded it was heavier still, but Hamer didn't plan to be carrying it far.

BONNIE AND CLYDE

Clyde and Buck Barrow grew up hard, in the pre-Depression Dallas of the 1920s, when almost every square mile of the plains had been broken by the plow, and agricultural prices were falling fast due to overproduction. Their family was one of the thousands of smallholders and sharecroppers driven off dry-land farms or laid off by landowning farmers. The frontier was closed, the rich rain-soaked lands of California and Oregon long taken. The movies were filled with the images of booming cities, big cars, and glittering nightlife, short-haired girls in slinky dresses smoking cigarettes and drinking champagne. There was none of that in drought-burned places like Telico, Texas, where Clyde Champion Barrow was born in 1909. But if rural life was stark and hungry, life in West Dallas, where the refugees from the dust and the economy gathered, was a meaner proposition. In 1922 the Barrow family lived under the Houston Street Viaduct, with other families in similar plight. It was there, as children, that Clyde would meet and befriend W. D. Jones, a future member of his gang. The part of West Dallas where they settled—the Eagle Ford area—was known then as the Devil's Back Porch.

Clyde's father Henry picked up scrap metal for sale, until a car ran over his mule and wagon. By 1927 Clyde and Buck Barrow were mostly thieves, starting with chickens, and graduating to cars. Bonnie Parker came to West Dallas with her sister Billie and widowed mother from Rowena,

During the early months of the robbery and killing spree, these two bold young people were in love with guns, robbery, and each other. Bonnie Parker loved the drama of the movies and had always been drawn to outlaws. In Clyde Barrow she found exactly what she was looking for. And she proved more than equal to the challenge of riding with him to the end.
Courtesy of the Texas Ranger Hall of Fame and Museum, Waco, TX

Texas, when Bonnie was still in elementary school. She was an excellent student, and fond of writing poetry in high school. Perhaps it was romanticism, or the free-for-all moral nature of the 1920s, or the contrast of those ideas with the rigid Baptist beliefs of her rural people that drew a very pretty young girl to the life of outlaws. Judging by the diaries she kept, she was a movie addict, and fond of whiskey and smoking Camel 20s. In 1926 when she was sixteen years old, she quit school to marry Roy Thornton, and had a double heart containing both of their names, tattooed on her right thigh. Thornton was a feckless small-time criminal, in Bonnie's words, "a roaming husband with a roaming mind." Their relationship was stormy when Thornton was around at all, and by 1929, a more mature Bonnie (she had already met Clyde Barrow) sent him on his way. It was a way that led to a sentence for murder at Eastham Prison Farm, where Thornton would be killed in an escape attempt in 1937, long after Bonnie was dead. The couple was never officially divorced. Bonnie was wearing his wedding ring when she was killed. Bonnie worked at Marco's Café in downtown Dallas until the Crash of 1929 put the restaurant out of business. Unemployed and living with a friend in West Dallas, she met Clyde Barrow, who was everything that Roy and her other many suitors could not have been: a deadly serious outlaw, and a man, who by all accounts, was her soul mate. She was nineteen, an inch less than five feet tall, weighing around one hundred pounds. Clyde was twenty-one years old, 5 feet 7, and weighed around 135. His wild life, especially in the ruins of an American economy that had marooned Bonnie and tens of thousands like her, must have seemed like everything she had ever wanted. He traveled constantly, robbing and burglarizing in a huge arc, as far north as Michigan, as far south as the Mexican border. He stole cars and wore suits in a time when most men were on foot and often in rags. The two young lovers became inseparable. Clyde was arrested for a burglary and held in the Waco jail in February of 1930. On a visit Bonnie smuggled a pistol in to him (it was said that she taped it below her breasts), and that night at suppertime, Clyde brandished the pistol at a guard and broke jail, running north to Illinois in a stolen V8 Ford. From there, he commenced a new, months-long robbery spree that landed him in jail in Ohio. He was extradited to face the charges in Waco. (Photos of Clyde Barrow from this time—including his mugshot from the arrest—show a man who looks like he is no more than seventeen, a promising boy, clean-cut, handsome, lean, extremely well dressed, and relaxed as ever.) He was sentenced to fourteen years at Eastham Prison Farm near Huntsville, Texas, for the burglary and the escape. Nobody, not Clyde, not even his mother Cumie, could say that the sentence was undeserved. Clyde was transported to Eastham by the legendary convict-hauler Uncle Bud Russell, in the armored cage on wheels that convicts called the One Way Wagon. Uncle Bud delivered Clyde into what must have been, for him, like one of the lowest circles of Hell. Clyde would say later that the prison was entirely corrupt, that men were beaten and left in sweat boxes for the smallest infractions, even that guards would murder obedient prisoners and then claim the $25 reward for stopping an escapee. Inmates were forced to work long hours on short rations, and a law of the jungle prevailed inside. Clyde—perhaps the smallest man there— became the victim of six-foot, two-hundred-pound "Big Ed" Crowder, thirty years old, a hardened convict from Houston, with connections—Ed was a building tender—that allowed him to move freely inside the prison. In October of 1931, Clyde put an end to Big Ed's depredations. The newspaper's cutlines read, HOUSTONIAN CUT 15 TIMES WITH HOMEMADE DIRK IN THE DIM LIGHT OF THE PRISON BARRACKS, and FIFTEEN STAB WOUNDS GIVEN VICTIM IN MINUTE AND HALF. Crowder died, and Clyde went to solitary. When he got out of the hole, he had a fellow convict chop off two of his toes with an axe, so he wouldn't have to go back to the brutal work in the cotton fields or on the chain gangs. Unknown to him, his mother Cumie had already attained a pardon for him, based, probably, on the well-recognized fact that Eastham was, indeed, a festering hole of inhumanity where a small twenty-one-year-old man could expect no more than to die or be enslaved. In February 1932, Clyde hobbled home to West Dallas, and to Bonnie, on crutches. He declared that he would never see the inside of a prison again, and that the "laws" as he called policemen, were his sworn enemies. Over

CLYDE CHAMPION BARROW

WANTED FOR MURDER

Notify

Sheriff's Office,
Dallas,Texas.

Age 27. Ht 5-7. Wt 125
Hair Dk. Blonde
Eyes Hazel.

F.P.C.
     29 - MO 9
     26 U 00 9

Courtesy of the Texas Ranger Hall of Fame and Museum, Waco, TX

Courtesy of the Texas Ranger Hall of Fame and Museum, Waco, TX

drinks of moonshine with outlaw friends he cleaned weapons and made elaborate plans for an attack on Eastham, and the liberation of the prisoners held there. Bonnie was never far from him. They stole cars and robbed small targets like rural grocery stores. A bank robber, Raymond Hamilton, joined them in their crimes, as did a rotating crew of badmen. Clyde (who was almost always the driver of the stolen V8 Fords) had an insatiable craving for distance. To drive a thousand miles from the scene of a crime to a tourist camp (there was no such thing as a motel then) or a secluded campsite in the woods of Louisiana or the thickets of the Trinity River was the norm for them. They sheltered in the waste places of the Ozarks, the Oklahoma badlands. They remained connected to family, and holed up in the Devil's Back Porch whenever they were home from the road, where they were safe from informants. Over the next two years, they committed dozens of robberies, and murdered twelve men, nine of whom were law officers. They kidnapped other officers—including the chief of police of Commerce, Louisiana—and released them unharmed. They photographed themselves endlessly, in a worship of weaponry and anarchic, V8 freedom, cigars and three-piece suits, hyperaware of their own status as hell-bent outlaws in a way that no Western gunman, not even Wild Bill Hickok in his fancy frontier clothes, ever approached. And their legend, through the headlines on newspapers starved by hard times for a good story, became outlandish. The Barrow Gang had no high-rolling nightlife, no bankrolls or diamonds. They were usually way out in the sticks, and their scores were small. Clyde and his brother Buck, when he joined the gang in 1933, didn't seem to care. But for hell-bent, very few outlaws have ever matched the two-year spree that ended in 1934. Clyde made good on a threat to attack Eastham Prison, breaking gang members, Raymond Hamilton, Henry Methvin, and three others out of jail, and covering their escape with a barrage of bullets, killing a guard. The gang was involved in five major gunfights with the law, always outnumbered.

But not outgunned. Clyde and Buck each had Browning Automatic Rifles that Clyde had heisted from a National Guard armory in Joplin, Missouri. Clyde's BAR (he called it his "scattergun") was sawed off and had a specially welded magazine that would hold over fifty rounds of .30–06 ammo. They used the BARs to devastating effect in three different fights with the law. Clyde kept a sixteen-gauge semiautomatic shotgun, "a whipit" as he called it, clipped to his right arm with a band of rubber innertube, under the sleeve of his suit coat. They had a lever-action ten-gauge shotgun, a Krag bolt-action rifle, and a host of other weapons of mayhem, blackjacks, knives, pistols. As W. D. "Deacon" Jones would say, in a 1968 interview in *Playboy* magazine,

> *I've seen that* Bonnie and Clyde *movie. The only thing that ain't plumb silly the way they play it is the gun battles. Them was real enough to almost make me hurt . . . When I tried to joining the Army in World War Two after I got out of prison, them doctors turned me down because*

*their X-rays showed four buckshot and a bullet in my chest and part of
a lung blown away.*

Jones was sixteen years old during the eight months he was riding with the
Barrow Gang. Buck Barrow died as result of wounds received in the July 1933
firefight at the Red Crown Tavern near Joplin, Missouri. His wife Blanche had
been blinded by flying glass in the fight and was captured following the next
major battle, with a posse at Dexter, Iowa. Bonnie was crippled by this time
as a result of a car wreck some months previous, where Clyde had flipped
their car to avoid driving off a collapsed bridge near Wellington, Texas. Her
legs had been badly burned by acid dripping from the car's battery while she
was pinned beneath it, and without real treatment, never healed. During the
Dexter fight, a badly wounded W. D. Jones dragged her across a small river to
escape, while Clyde, shot through the leg, and bleeding from a ricochet to the
side of the head, held the posse off with bursts from his customized BAR scattergun. They just barely managed to escape in a stolen car. They were clearly
running out of time.

TIME RUNS OUT

It was Lee Simmons, chief of the Texas prison system, who decided it had
gone on long enough. Simmons was outraged by the Eastham break and the
killing of the guard. And there was little doubt that the idea that the Barrow
Gang were folk heroes was galling to law enforcement officers everywhere.
Bonnie's poems and the many photos of the gang's antics had been published
in newspapers far and wide, along with tales of epic battles and heists, cast
before the hungry eyes of a nation with nine million unemployed males, and
soup lines in every major city. It was dangerously subversive.

On February 1, 1934, Simmons traveled to Austin to ask Frank Hamer,
then fifty years old and working as an investigator for an oil company, to track
Bonnie and Clyde. It would take Hamer 102 days to find and kill them. Hamer
would tell the Ranger historian Walter Prescott Webb: "Before the chase was

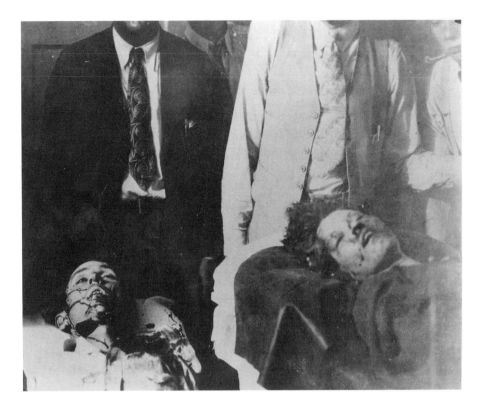

On the run, hiding out, and always preparing for battle, Barrow gang member W. D. Jones said it best, "Bonnie was like Clyde. They had grit. They meant to stay free or go down together."

Courtesy of the Texas Ranger Hall of Fame and Museum, Waco, TX

over, I not only knew the general appearance and mental habits of the pair, but I also learned the kind of whiskey that they drank, what they ate, and the size, texture and color of their clothes. I first struck their trail at Texarkana . . . near Keechi, they went in the night to a negro house and had the negroes cook them some cornbread and fry a chicken . . . But the trail always led back to Louisiana." Hamer found a "mailbox," a place where the gang left each other messages, beneath an old board by the highway, near Gibsland, Louisiana. Bob Alcorn and Ted Hinton joined Hamer to set up an ambush at the site of the "mailbox." B. M. Gault, a former Texas Ranger, had been helping

Hamer trail the Barrows for almost a month. Hamer informed Bienville Parish sheriff Henderson Jordan and his deputy, Prentiss Oakley, of the plan, and they joined the ambush team. They set up in the middle of the night on May 22, overlooking the "mailbox" and well concealed in the brush—Hamer, with his Model 8, Gault, Sheriff Jordan, Alcorn, Prentiss Oakley, also armed with Model 8s, and twenty-seven-year-old Ted Hinton, the youngest member of the team, armed with a Colt Monitor .30–06, a weapon almost as fearsome as the BARs they hoped not to face in Barrow's hands.

Barrow's V8 Ford came into view at almost nine in the morning. Hamer would say that the car was traveling at such high speed that he could hear it "singing like a sewing machine." The sun was up and at the lawmen's backs when the car came to a stop, in the exact spot that Hamer had chosen. Hamer claims that someone commanded, "Stick 'em up!" and that Bonnie and Clyde immediately reached for their weapons. It could well have been true. Whatever the preliminaries, the lawmen opened fire, Hamer working the "pear burner" for all it was worth. One of the ambush team would later recall that Bonnie "screamed like a panther" when the barrage began. Both Bonnie and Clyde were rocked with bullets, in the torso, their faces, heads. The spree was over. In the gore of the car, among scattered cigarette packs, the lawmen would find the Barrow arsenal: three BARS, the sawed off ten-gauge lever-action, a sawed-off twenty-gauge, seven Colt 1911s in .45, other weapons, and three thousand rounds of ammunition. The Model 8 that Frank Hamer used on that day is in private hands (most experts agree that Hamer's engraved Model 8 .30 caliber at the Texas Ranger Museum was not the one he used in the ambush, although Boot Hinton—ambush team member Ted Hinton's son—says that he believes that it was). It was passed down to Frank Hamer Jr. at some point. Prentiss Oakley's Model 8, which he had borrowed for the ambush from a dentist in Arcadia, Louisiana, and which may have fired the first rounds of the ambush fusillade, has changed hands at least twice since the deaths of Bonnie and Clyde—the last time, Boot Hinton believes, it sold at auction for over $140,000. Clyde Barrow's BARs, his sawed-off sixteen-gauge coat gun, and other guns from the death car are on display near Frank Hamer's engraved .30 Model 8. The rifle that stop-car man Ted Hinton was shooting, the fearsome Colt Monitor .30–06, is there, too. They sit there behind glass, tools of violence from a hard and bygone era, variously steeped in rage, or in righteousness, the sweat of adrenaline or terror darkening their wood and etching their steel. For those who truly know their stories, of the men and women who used them, they glow there like the old embers of a fire that will never go out.

BIBLIOGRAPHY

Chapter One: John Brown's Sharps Model 1850 Sporting Rifle

Abels, Jules. *Man on Fire: John Brown and the Cause of Liberty.* New York: MacMillan, 1971.

Avery, Elijah. *The Capture and Execution of John Brown.* Chicago: Afro-American Press, 1969.

Barton, O. S. *Three Years with Quantrill.* Norman and London: University of Oklahoma Press, 1992.

Chapel, Charles E. *Guns of the Old West.* New York: Coward-McCann, 1961.

Frank, Tom. *What's the Matter with Kansas? How Conservatives Won the Heart of America.* New York: Metropolitan Books, 2004.

Garraty, John A. *The American Nation: A History of the United States to 1877.* New York: Harper and Row, 1966.

"John Brown (abolitionist)." http://en.wikipedia.org/wiki/John_Brown_%28abolitionist%29.

Kansas City Kansas Community College, copies of the *Squatter Sovereign* posted online, www.kckcc.edu/pdfs/academics/social-science/territorial_news/squatter_sovereign/s2s24a.pdf.

Ortner, Eric, "A Legend Grows While Revolutionizing Small Arms," www.snipersparadise.com/history/sharps.htm.

Schultz, Duane. *Quantrill's War: The Life and Times of William Clark Quantrill.* New York: St. Martin's, 1996.

"Sharps Rifle." http://en.wikipedia.org/wiki/Sharps_Rifle.

Worman, Charles G. *Gunsmoke and Saddleleather: Firearms in the Nineteenth Century American West.* Albuquerque: University of New Mexico Press, 2005.

Chapter Two: James Butler "Wild Bill" Hickok's Colt Model 1851 Revolvers

"Colt 1851 Navy Revolver." http://en.wikipedia.org/wiki/Colt_1851_Navy_Revolver.

"Colt Dragoon Revolver." http://en.wikipedia.org/wiki/Colt_Dragoon_Revolver.

Hackman, Emory, and Linda Adams, "Common Guns in the Civil War: Colt Model 1851 Revolver," www.hackman-adams.com/guns/colt36.htm.

"Jack McCall." http://en.wikipedia.org/wiki/Jack_McCall.

Kennedy, David. *Guns of the Wild West: A Photographic Tour of the Guns That Shaped Our Country's History.* Philadelphia: Running Press, 2005.

O'Connor, Richard. *Wild Bill Hickok: A Biography of James Butler Hickok, the West's Greatest Gunfighter.* New York: Doubleday, 1959.

O'Neal, Bill. *An Encyclopedia of Western Gunfighters.* Norman: University of Oklahoma Press, 1979.

"Richard Francis Burton." http://en.wikipedia.org/wiki/Richard_Francis_Burton.

Rosa, Joseph G. *They Called Him Wild Bill.* Norman: University of Oklahoma Press, 1964.

Stroud, David, "Guns of the Texas Rangers: The Colt Navy," *Texas Ranger Dispatch Magazine,* www.texasranger.org/dispatch/4/ColtNavy.htm.

"Wild Bill Hickok." http://en.wikipedia.org/wiki/Wild_Bill_Hickok.

Worman, Charles G. *Gunsmoke and Saddle Leather: Firearms in the Nineteenth-Century American West.* Albuquerque: University of New Mexico Press, 2005.

Chapter Three: William "Buffalo Bill" Cody's Springfield Model 1863 Rifle

Accurate, ".50–70 Government," www.accuratepowder.com/data/PerCaliber2Guide/Rifle/ObsoleteCartridges/50%2070%20Government%20page%20366%20to%20367.pdf.

Brown, Dee. *Bury My Heart at Wounded Knee.* New York: Bantam Books, 1970.

Cody, William F. *The Life of Buffalo Bill Cody.* Hartford, Conn.: F. E. Bliss, 1879.

Durham, Kenny. "The .50–70 Government: America's First Big-Bore Centerfire," *Shoot! Magazine,* www.shootmagazine.com/articles/firearms/50-70_govt.htm.

Kennedy, David. Guns of the Wild West: A Photographic Tour of the Guns That Shaped Our Country's History. Philadelphia: Running Press, 2005.

Russell, Don. *The Lives and Legends of Buffalo Bill.* Norman: University of Oklahoma Press, 1960.

Sorg, Eric. *Buffalo Bill: Myth and Reality.* Santa Fe, N.M.: Ancient City Press, 1998.

The U.S. Springfield Trapdoor Rifle Information Center. www.trapdoor collector.com.

"Wagon Box Fight." http://en.wikipedia.org/wiki/Wagon_Box_Fight.

Worman, Charles G. *Gunsmoke and Saddle Leather: Firearms in the Nineteenth-Century American West.* Albuquerque: University of New Mexico Press, 2005.

Chapter Four: Geronimo's Winchester Model 1876 Carbine

"Apache Wars." http://en.wikipedia.org/wiki/Apache_Wars.

Ball, Eve. *In the Days of Victorio: Recollections of a Warm Springs Apache.* Narrated by James Kayawaykla. Tucson: University of Arizona Press, 1970.

Brown, Dee. *Bury My Heart at Wounded Knee.* New York: Bantam Books, 1970.

Carter, Forrest. *Watch for Me on the Mountain.* New York: Delacorte Press, 1978.

"The Chiricahua Apaches: Cochise, Geronimo and Mangas Coloradas," Desert USA, www.desertusa.com/magfeb98/feb_pap/du_apache.html.

"Cochise." http://en.wikipedia.org/wiki/Cochise.

Conservator's Report National Museum of the American Indian (Courtesy of NMAI).

Flayderman, Norm. *Flayderman's Guide to Antique Firearms.* 8th ed. Iola, Wisc.: Krause Publications, 2001.

"Geronimo." http://en.wikipedia.org/wiki/Geronimo.

Horn, Tom. *The Life of Tom Horn, Written by Himself.* Norman: University of Oklahoma Press, 1964.

"Lozen." http://en.wikipedia.org/wiki/Lozen.

"Lozen, Apache Warrior." www.lozen.net.

"Mangas Coloradas." http://en.wikipedia.org/wiki/Mangas_Coloradas.

Sharp, J. W., "The Apache People of the Southwestern Deserts," *Desert USA,* www.desertusa.com/ind1/du_peo_apache.html.

———. "Cochise and the Bascom Affair," The Apache People of the Southwestern Deserts, *Desert USA,* www.desertusa.com/ind1/Cochise.html.

"Victorio." http://en.wikipedia.org/wiki/Victorio.

Welker, Glenn. "Geronimo: Goyathlay ("one who yawns")," www.indians.org/welker/geronimo.htm.

Wilson, R. L. *Winchester: An American Legend.* Edison, N.J.: Chartwell Books, 1991.

Worman, Charles G. *Gunsmoke and Saddle Leather: Firearms in the Nineteenth-Century American West.* Albuquerque: University of New Mexico Press, 2005.

Chapter Five: Joseph Smith's Ethan Allen Dragoon Model Pepperbox Pistol

Bentley, Joseph I. Martyrdom of Joseph Smith, Light Planet. www.lightplanet.com/mormons/people/joseph_smith/martyrdom.html.

Bushman, Richard L. *Joseph Smith: Rough Stone Rolling.* New York: Alfred A. Knopf, 2005.

Chapel, Charles E. *Guns of the Old West.* New York: Coward-McCann, 1961.

"Cyrus H. Wheelock." http://en.wikipedia.org/wiki/Cyrus_H._Wheelock.

Daniels, William M. "Correct Account of the murder of General Joseph and Hyrum Smith at Carthage on the 27th Day of June, 1844." 1845. F550 m8 D18 1845. www.wiu.edu/library/units/archives/archives_web.sphp?id=210.

"Danite." http://en.wikipedia.org/wiki/Danite.

"Extermination Order." http://en.wikipedia.org/wiki/Extermination_Order.

Flanders, Robert B. "Dream and Nightmare: Nauvoo Revisited." In *The Restoration Movement: Essays in Mormon History,* edited by F. Mark McKiernan, Alma R. Blair, and Paul M. Edwards. Lawrence, Kans.: Coronado Press, 1973. 141–66.

———. *Nauvoo: Kingdom on the Mississippi.* Urbana: University of Illinois, 1965.

Hay, John. "The Mormon Prophet's Tragedy," *Atlantic Monthly,* December 1869, www.utlm.org/onlineresources/johnhayarticle.htm.

Jennings, Warren. "The City in the Garden: Social Conflict in Jackson County, Missouri." In *The Restoration Movement: Essays in Mormon History,* edited by F. Mark McKiernan, Alma R. Blair, and Paul M. Edwards. Lawrence, Kans.: Coronado Press, 1973. 99–119.

"Joseph Smith Jr." http://en.wikipedia.org/wiki/Joseph_Smith_Jr.

Kennedy, David. *Guns of the Wild West: A Photographic Tour of the Guns That Shaped Our Country's History.* Philadelphia: Running Press, 2005.

"Lilburn Boggs." http://en.wikipedia.org/wiki/Lilburn_Boggs.

"Mormon War." http://en.wikipedia.org/wiki/Mormon_War.

"Nauvoo Expositor." http://en.wikipedia.org/wiki/Nauvoo_Expositor.

Schindler, Harold. *Orrin Porter Rockwell: Son of God, Man of Thunder.* Salt Lake City: University of Utah Press, 1966.

William Law (Latter Day Saints). http://en.wikipedia.org/wiki/William_Law_%28Latter_Day_Saints%29.

Worman, Charles G. *Gunsmoke and Saddle Leather: Firearms in the Nineteenth-Century American West.* Albuquerque: University of New Mexico Press, 2005.

Wyckoff, James. *Famous Guns That Won the West.* New York: Arco Publishing, 1975.

Chapter Six: Chief Joseph's "Surrender Gun"—Model 1866 Winchester Rifle

Brown, Dee. *Bury My Heart at Wounded Knee.* New York: Bantam Books, 1970.

Howard, Helen A. *Saga of Chief Joseph.* Caldwell, Idaho: Caxton Printers, 1941.

Josephy, Alvin M. Jr. *The Nez Percé Indians and the Opening of the Northwest.* Abridged edition. Lincoln: University of Nebraska Press, 1965.

Wilson, R. L. *Winchester: An American Legend.* Edison, N.J.: Chartwell Books, 1991.

Worman, Charles G. *Gunsmoke and Saddle Leather: Firearms in the Nineteenth-Century American West.* Albuquerque: University of New Mexico Press, 2005.

Chapter Seven: Ned Christie's Model 1873 Winchester Rifle

Cherokee Nation, Cultural Resource Center, "Ned Christie Story: Cherokee Senator—Patriot—Martyr-Blacksmith—Farmer—Marble Champion." www.yvwiiusdinvnohii.net/Cherokee/NedChristieStory.htm.

Conley, Robert J. *The Witch of Going Snake and Other Stories.* Norman: University of Oklahoma Press, 1988.

Flayderman, Norm. *Flayderman's Guide to Antique Firearms.* 8th ed. Iola, Wis.: Krause Publications, 2001.

Garraty, John A. *The American Nation: A History of the United States to 1877.* New York: Harper and Row, 1966.

O'Neal, Bill. *An Encyclopedia of Western Gunfighters.* Norman: University of Oklahoma Press, 1979.

Shirley, Glenn. *West of Hell's Fringe: Crime, Criminals, and the Federal Peace Officer in Oklahoma Territory.* Norman: University of Oklahoma Press, 1978.

Speer, Bonnie. *"Ned Christie: Cherokee Outlaw."* www.historynet.com/magazines/wild_west/3026941.html.

Wilson, R. L. *Winchester: An American Legend.* Edison, N.J.: Chartwell Books, 1991.

Chapter Eight: John Wesley Hardin's Colt Double Action Revolvers Model 1877

"The Armchair Gunshow." Colt Model 1877 DA Lightnings and Thunderers, and 1878 Double Action Revolvers For Sale**.** www.armchairgunshow.com/otsCD_Colt_1877_1878.htm.

Chapel, Charles E. *Guns of the Old West.* New York: Coward-McCann, 1961.

"Colt Lightning." http://en.wikipedia.org/wiki/Colt_Lightning

"Colt Single Action Army." http://en.wikipedia.org/wiki/Colt_Single_Action_Army.

Hardin, John W. Gunfighter: *The Autobiography of John Wesley Hardin.* Washington, D.C.: Creation Books, 2001. First published as *The Life of John Wesley Hardin as Written by Himself.* 1896 by Smith and Moore.

"How I got Started with the 41 Long Colt." www.dnmsport.com/41LC/41%20LONG%20COLT.htm.

Huntington, Jim. "John Wesley Hardin's Death Gun." *American Handgunner Magazine,* November–December 2002.

"John Wesley Hardin." http://en.wikipedia.org/wiki/John_Wesley_Hardin.

Metz, Leon. *John Wesley Hardin: Dark Angel of Texas.* Norman: University of Oklahoma Press, 1996.

O'Neal, Bill. *An Encyclopedia of Western Gunfighters.* Norman: University of Oklahoma Press, 1979.

"Robert Adams (Handgun Designer)." http://en.wikipedia.org/wiki/
   Robert_Adams_of_London.

Velleux, David L. "U.S. Revolver Models 1889, 1892, 1894, 1895 and 1896,"
   The Spanish American War Centennial Web site, www.spanamwar.com/
   Colt1889series.htm.

Worman, Charles G. *Gunsmoke and Saddle Leather: Firearms in the
   Nineteenth-Century American West.* Albuquerque: University of New
   Mexico Press, 2005.

Chapter Nine: Tom Horn's Winchester Model 1894 Rifle

Carlson, Chip. *Tom Horn: Blood on the Moon: Dark History of the Mysterious
   Cattle Detective.* Glendo, Wyo.: High Plains Press, 2001.

———. "Tom Horn's Story." www.tom-horn.com.

Flayderman, Norm. *Flayderman's Guide to Antique Firearms.* 8th ed. Iola,
   Wis.: Krause Publications, 2001.

Garavaglia, Luis A., and Charles G. Worman. *Firearms of the American West
   1866–1894.* Albuquerque: University of New Mexico Press, 1985.

Horan, James D. *The Gunfighters: The Authentic Wild West.* New York: Crown
   Publishers, 1976.

Horn, Tom. *Life of Tom Horn: Government Scout and Interpreter.* Norman:
   University of Oklahoma Press, 1964.

"The Murder of Willie Nickell, Joe LeFors and the Confession of Horn,
   Horn's Trial," "Tom Horn: From Wyoming Tales and Trails," www
   .wyomingtalesandtrails.com/horn2.html.

O'Neal, Bill. *An Encyclopedia of Western Gunfighters.* Norman: University of
   Oklahoma Press, 1979.

Rosa, Joseph G. *The Taming of the West: Age of the Gunfighter.* New York:
   Smithmark Publishers, 1993.

"A Saga of the West." http://nickell.tierranet.com/tales/kels.htm.

Wilson, R. L. *Winchester: An American Legend.* Edison, N.J.: Chartwell Books, 1991.

Worman, Charles G. *Gunsmoke and Saddle Leather: Firearms in the Nineteenth-Century American West.* Albuquerque: University of New Mexico Press, 2005.

Chapter Ten: William "Bill" Tilghman Jr.'s Colt Single Action Army Revolvers

"Cattle Annie and Little Britches." www.theoutlaws.com/outlaws2.htm.

Chapel, Charles E. *Guns of the Old West:* New York: Coward-McCann, 1961.

Haven, Charles T., and Frank A. Belden. *A History of the Colt Revolver and the Other Arms Made by Colt's Patent Fire Arms Manufacturing Company from 1836–1940.* New York: Bonanza Books, 1940.

O'Neal, Bill. *An Encyclopedia of Western Gunfighters.* Norman: University of Oklahoma Press, 1979.

Shirley, Glenn. *West of Hell's Fringe: Crime, Criminals, and the Federal Peace Officer in Oklahoma Territory.* Norman: University of Oklahoma Press, 1978.

Tilghman, G. Wayne. "The Long Trail that ended in Cromwell: the Life and Death of Legendary Lawman Bill Tilghman," www.rootsweb.ancestry .com/~oklincol/tilghman/tilghman.htm.

Venturino, Mike. "The Twentieth Century Peacemaker," *Shooting Times,* November 1999, www.galleryofguns.com/Shootingtimes/Articles/ DisplayArticles.asp?ID=19.

Wellman, Paul I. *A Dynasty of Western Outlaws.* Lincoln: University of Nebraska Press, 1961.

Worman, Charles G. *Gunsmoke and Saddle Leather: Firearms in the Nineteenth-Century American West.* Albuquerque: University of New Mexico Press, 2005.

Chapter Eleven: Pancho Villa's Smith & Wesson Model 3 American Revolver

"Artillery in the Mexican Revolution," www.latinamericanstudies.org/mexican-artillery.htm.

Associated Press, "Two guns owned by Mexican folk hero Pancho Villa Up for Auction," dallasnews.com, November 7, 2007, www.dallasnews.com/sharedcontent/dws/dn/latestnews/stories/110807dntexvillaguns.1e97f581e.html.

Atkin, Ronald. *Revolution.* New York: John Day Company, 1969.

Brecher, Gary. "Celaya Machismo Versus Overlapping Fields of Fire," *The Exile,* June 29, 2006, www.exile.ru/articles/detail.php?ARTICLE_ID=8223&IBLOCK_ID=35.

Brenner, Anita, and George R. Leighton. *The Wind That Swept Mexico.* Austin: University of Texas Press, 1943.

Gilliam, Ronald. R. "Mexican Revolution: Battle of Celaya," HistoryNet.com, www.historynet.com/magazines/mhq/3027751.html.

Machado, Manuel A. Jr. *Centaur of the North.* Austin, Tex.: Eakin Press, 1988.

Stewart, Christopher R. "Pancho Villa's Munitions." Master's thesis, University of Montana, 1979.

Tuolumne Lawman, SASS #6127, "Smith & Wesson's #3, Colt's Biggest Rival in the Old West," www.sam-hane.com/sass/schofield/history.htm.

Venturino, Mike, "American legends: those fantastic .44s!" American Handgunner, Sept–Oct, 2005, http://findarticles.com/p/articles/mi_m0BTT/is_177_29/ai_n14816289.

Wilson, Jim, "Guns of the Mexican Revolution," www.shootingtimes.com/gunsmoke/professionals_0731.

Chapter Twelve: Frank Hamer's Remington Model 8 Semi-Auto

Ballinger, Frank R. Internet resources and e-mail communications. "Bonnie and Clyde's Hideout." http://texashideout.tripod.com/huntsville.html.

Boot Hinton, Bonnie and Clyde Ambush Museum, interview.

Case, Timothy, "Hallmark of innovation: The Remington Model Eight: Old fashioned doesn't necessarily mean obsolete. The sleek Remington Model 8 is still fit for the game trails," *Guns Magazine,* May 2002, http://findarticles.com/p/articles/mi_m0BQY/is_5_48/ai_84145944.

"Firearm Model History," http://www.remington.com/pages/our-company/Company-History.aspx.

Garraty, John A. *The American Nation, A History of the United States Since 1865.* New York: Harper and Row, 1966.

Jenkins, John H., and H. Gordon Frost. *"I'm Frank Hamer."* Austin, Tex: Statehouse Press, 1968.

Vasto, Mark. "Bonnie, Clyde and the Battle of Platte County," *The Landmark: Platte County Newspaper,* www.plattecountylandmark.com/Bonnieandclyde.htm.

ABOUT THE AUTHOR

Hal Herring is a contributing editor at *Field & Stream* and an editor at large for *New West,* a publication covering issues around the Rocky Mountain states. He grew up in Alabama, in the company of good guns and great storytellers, and has been involved in the shooting sports since childhood. He lives at the edge of the Rockies, in the windy little town of Augusta, Montana, with his wife and two children.